O9-AIG-090

ANGELS
IN OUR
TIME

ISHVARA D'ANGELO

First published by O Books, 2006
An imprint of John Hunt Publishing Ltd.,
The Bothy, Deershot Lodge, Park Lane,
Ropley, Hants, SO24 0BE, UK
office@johnhunt-publishing.com
www.o-books.net

USA and Canada
NBN
custserv@nbnbooks.com
Tel: 1 800 462 6420 Fax: 1 800 338 4550

Australia
Brumby Books
sales@brumbybooks.com
Tel: 61 3 9761 5535 Fax: 61 3 9761 7095

New Zealand: Peaceful Living
books@peaceful-living.co.nz
Tel: 64 7 57 18105 Fax: 61 3 9761 7095

Singapore
STP
davidbuckland@tlp.com.sg
Tel: 65 6276 Fax: 65 6276 7119

South Africa
Alternative Books
altbook@peterhyde.ca.za
Tel: 27 21447 5300 Fax: 27 21447 1430

Text and illustrations copyright Ishvara d'Angelo 2006

Design: Stuart Davies

ISBN-13: 978 1 905047 87 1
ISBN-10: 1 905047 87 8

All rights reserved. Except for brief quotations in
critical articles or reviews, no part of this book may
be reproduced in any manner without prior written
permission from the publishers.

The rights of Ishvara d'Angelo as author have been
asserted in accordance with the Copyright, Designs
and Patents Act 1988.

A CIP catalogue record for this book is available from
the British Library.

Printed by Maple-Vail, USA

ANGELS
IN OUR
TIME

ISHVARA D'ANGELO

BOOKS

Winchester, UK
Washington, USA

CONTENTS

Acknowledgments   vii

PART 1: THINKING ABOUT ANGELS   1

Why Angels? Why Now?   2

One Woman's Journey   10

The Nature of Angels   16

What do Angels Look Like?   21

Angel Families and Angel Work   26

Guardian Angels   31

PART 2: ARCHANGELS IN OUR TIME   37

Gabriel, The Herald of Change   39

Michael, The Commander   43

Raphael, The Healer   50

Uriel, the Guardian of Earth   56

Some Other Archangels   61

PART 3: WORKING WITH ANGELS   67

On Seeing Angels   71

Prayer and Meditation   78

Journaling with Angels   81

Angel Cards and Oracles   86

Channeling with the Angels   90

Angels and Creativity   93

When Bad Things Happen   98

Working with Archangel Gabriel   101

Working with Archangel Michael   103

Working with Archangel Raphael   106

Working with Archangel Uriel   110

PART 4: ANGEL MESSAGES   115

The Angel of Abundance   119

The Angel of Creativity   119

The Angel of Responsibility   120

The Angel of Gentleness   120

The Angel of Speed   121

The Angel of Rest   123

The Angel of Hope   123

The Angel of Simplicity   124

APPENDIX: Useful contacts   127

Bibliography and suggested further reading   129

ACKNOWLEDGMENTS

This book could not have been written without the help and support of many human friends, as well as all my unseen helpers, and I want to thank David Cousins and Mary Hykel-Hunt for their workshops, Solara and Theolyn Cortens for their workshops and books, Liz Dolton for angelic healing sessions and Richard Offutt for healing and many very powerful insights. Special thanks to Evelyn Burges, Annie Lloyd and Bebe Swanson for their unflagging encouragement and to all the people who have shared their personal experiences of angels with me: those whose stories do not appear in the book contributed just as much as those whose experiences you will find in these pages. Thanks also to Karen Kay for having first given me the opportunity to present these ideas in talks and workshops. Last but by no means least, thank you to John Hunt for being a sensitive and supportive publisher. None of this would have been possible without them.

PART ONE

THINKING ABOUT ANGELS

WHY ANGELS?
WHY NOW?

The Angels keep their ancient places,
Turn but a stone and start a wing.
'Tis ye, 'tis your estranged faces
That miss the many-splendoured thing.

FRANCIS THOMPSON from *The Kingdom of God*

Angels are all around us. You will find them at every turn. There are talks and workshops about them, web-sites devoted to them, books, TV programmes and newspaper articles about them and courses of study offering to increase your awareness and understanding of them.

You can buy Angel cards and tee-shirts, Angel pins or earrings, candles, mirrors, dolls and every imaginable kind of merchandise.

Clearly, none of these things is really an Angel, but they reflect the huge and growing interest in Angels at this time. In fact, there has not been so much focus on Angels at any time since the Middle Ages. So, where have the Angels been all this time? Why this sudden resurgence?

In fact the Angels have never left us: it is our awareness of them that has been dormant for so long. The poet Francis Thompson expressed it perfectly in the verse that heads this chapter. More and more, though, we are not missing the splendor of the Angels and Archangels. The results of opinion polls suggest that more than 60% of people in Great Britain and America believe in Angels, and many of those people say that they have experienced the presence of Angels. All sorts of people from mystics to "ordinary" people in the street, report seeing Angels, hearing them, being helped by them in times of crisis or healed by them when desperately ill and, significantly, many of those people had no belief or interest in Angels before such an encounter. This was true of my own first experience of an Angel and you will find a number of other personal stories that echo that throughout this book. At first sight, this may seem surprising, since life now is so different from life six or seven hundred years ago: after all, we live in the age of reason, not to say skepticism, of mass communication, rapid transport, space exploration and global businesses. We have split the atom and put men on the Moon, we have produced genetically modified plants and cloned animals, we have exploited and polluted our Planet to within a hair's-breadth of catastrophe.

Earth is not the innocent place it was in the fourteenth century. And yet, there are parallels.

Mediaeval Europe was racked by endless wars, there was widespread famine and there was the Black Death. In fact, these three horrors were not separate entities but intimately connected; the waves of bubonic plague that swept the continent of Europe decimated populations that were already weakened by decades of malnutrition, and the hunger was often due to the diversion of men and resources from farming to fighting - whether in local quarrels, inter-state wars or the succession of Crusades.

It doesn't take a huge leap of imagination to see the similarities between then and now if we look at the world as a whole, rather than Europe alone.

Barely a day passes without distressing news of war, famine or disease. The wealthy nations spend immeasurable resources on war, while there is famine in much of the undeveloped world. There is the global plague of Aids, as well as other diseases that can spread from continent to continent with frightening speed because of the ease of international travel. Just as in mediaeval Europe, these facts are not unconnected; much of the hunger is a direct result of local wars, particularly in Africa. There too, a famine-stricken population has less resistance to illness, both Aids and other infections, and though some politicians may think it too simplistic to say so, if a fraction of the resources currently expended on making war were to be spent on food, health education, medicines and medical care, millions of lives could be saved.

But, beyond these parallels, there is a new factor: the very real danger that we are destroying the very Planet we live on.

So, is this new wave of interest in Angels merely a reaction to distressing conditions? Is it just something comforting to hang on to in difficult times? I don't think so: I think it is more that these messengers of the Divine are asking us to wake up, to take spiritual responsibility for what is happening in our world, to work in partnership with them and actively DO something about it.

But why did we lose sight of them for hundreds of years?

One reason is certainly the rise of humanism during the early Renaissance: writers and thinkers became more interested in human behavior, history and philosophy than in any manifestation of the Divine.

A more potent reason, and one which affected far more people was the Reformation: the new-born Protestant churches had far less sympathy with mystics and visionaries than the older Catholic church from which they had seceded, though the Catholic church itself became far more rigid over the years. There came a time when to admit to having seen or heard an Angel was more likely to lead to an Auto da Fe than to canonization!

This did not mean that people did not hear or see or otherwise experience Angels: it meant that they became cautious about discussing their experiences openly. Writers would hesitate before mentioning any personal experience of Angels in their work, painters were commissioned to portray figures from classical mythology rather than saints, Angels or the Madonna.

Even the way that Angels were depicted, when they did appear in art, moved towards fat little babies rather than the beautiful and often awe-inspiring figures of an earlier generation.

Writers and painters respond to the outlook of the society they live in, but they help to shape it, too. If Angels are not spoken of, if people no longer see representations of Angels around them, it is easy for them to slip from general consciousness.

The eighteenth century "Enlightenment" further distanced thoughts of Angels from many minds. The emphasis was on logic, science and fact and many of the major minds of that time denied the existence of anything beyond the earthly plane.

Of course, in every age there have been exceptions: great geniuses like William Blake or Francis Thompson and ordinary men and woman about whom we know nothing, but they are not representative of the society they lived in.

In many ways, we have become even more divorced from the Divine in the last hundred years. All the scientific discoveries of the twentieth century have placed huge emphasis on the material rather than the spiritual and the mass media exaggerates this.

Conversely, though, new developments in physics have changed our understanding of the way the universe functions and made it easier for us to envisage discarnate Beings suddenly materializing, and if we suspect that time is not a linear process we can accept more readily that the same Angel can appear in more than one place at the same time. For many people, the church and religious practices seem to have no relevance to their daily lives. Paradoxically, though, widespread disillusion with established religion has created the conditions in which it is easier for the Angels to make themselves known to us. Many people who no longer feel comfortable within any church but continue to believe in a Divine Spirit are finding new ways to worship, which may range from solitary practice through small, less formal religious groupings, to an approach to Spirit that has been labeled "New Age" though that in itself embraces a huge variety of avenues. The practice of meditation has been popularized by an interest in Eastern religions and absorbed into many other beliefs and this in itself has enabled many people to access direct experience of Angels.

Admittedly, there is a certain trivialization and commercialization of the renewed interest in Angels: a plethora of Angel-related dolls, figurines, brooches and the like.

But it is not the Angels that we trivialize, it is ourselves. They remain what they have always been, just as they were ever-present even when humanity as a whole ignored them.

If we don't move beyond the superficial, if we fall into a too-easy belief that just acknowledging the existence of Angels is all we have to do, if we are not prepared to do some real work in co-operation with them, then we miss the opportunity to vastly enrich our lives.

Another danger lies in a tendency to worship Angels as entities in their own right and not as messengers of the Divine. For the Angels are messengers: their very name comes from the Greek word for messenger. They are traditionally called Messengers of God though I prefer to call them Messengers of the Divine because Angels transcend all religions and belief systems. We should not, though, fall into the error of thinking of them as separate from a Divine Intelligence, whatever name we choose to give to that Intelligence, or of worshipping them. They are messengers, agents, representatives of the Divine on Earth. They cannot act without the Divine; it is debatable how much autonomy they have. In fact they would not exist without the Divine.

There are many ways of approaching the Divine, and you alone know which of them is the right one for you. But whichever that is, if you embrace the Angels as a way of bringing Spirit into your life, I invite you to come with me on a journey through this book and hope that it will, in some small way, enhance your understanding of these glorious Beings.

A MEDITATION

Before you attempt the following meditation or any of the meditations in this book, please read the following notes on meditation in general. Once you have done so, will embark on a journey together.

You may already be an experienced meditator, in which case you will already have your own preferred way of doing things; you will probably have a favorite place to sit, you will know what time of day is best suited to meditation for you, you will know how to create a feeling of calm before you embark on the meditation itself. In that case, please ignore what follows and use the meditations in the book in the way that works best for you.

If you are not experienced in this field, though, please spend a little time reading the following suggestions which I hope will help you get the maximum benefit from the meditations that I have suggested.

First, find a time and a place where you will not be disturbed. If you live in a busy household this may be late at night, or early in the morning before others are awake. If you have school-age children, you may want to set aside some time for meditation while they are at school. Alternatively, you may need to make a "Do Not Disturb" sign and ask the people around you to respect your need to be quiet for a little while. Remember to turn off all telephones - both mobile and landline.

Some people like to sit or kneel on the floor, perhaps supported by cushions, while others prefer to sit on a chair. Choose whichever feels most comfortable to you because if you are not comfortable, you are likely to be distracted from your meditation. Sit with your spine as straight as possible and both feet firmly on the floor. Close your eyes and focus on each area of your body in turn, starting with your feet and working upwards. Is any area tense? Take a few moments to relax any tight muscles. A simple way to do so is to screw them up, make them even tighter, and then let go - breathing out as you do so.

Now focus on your breathing, feeling the breath enter your nose and leave it, the gentle rise and fall of your chest as it does so. Go on doing this until you feel calm and relaxed, then begin the meditation or visualization.

Some people find it useful to record the suggestions rather than try to memories them. If you think this will help, record the meditations and play them back very quietly whenever you want to.

Be gentle with yourself after any meditation. Take a few deep breaths, stretch gently, feel your feet firmly in contact with the floor before you get up from your sitting position. Try, if possible, not to rush into your day-to-day activities too quickly. You may want to eat or drink something, as this has a grounding effect, bringing you back to Earth very effectively.

A JOURNEY THROUGH TIME

Make yourself comfortable and spend a little time breathing quietly before we set out on a journey through time.

Close your eyes and imagine that you are present on this Earth at some time in the past. You are in a place that you know well in the present, but it is subtly different: the first thing you notice is how quiet it is, there are no cars, no planes overhead, no mobile phones though after a while you become aware of the sounds of hammering, sawing, horses' hoofs, perhaps a mill-wheel turning. You notice that people's clothes are very different, some of the familiar old buildings are there but perhaps look quite new. But beyond the physical, the look, the sound, the smell of the place, you are strongly aware of the presence of Angels, many of them, moving among and above the people, the houses and the animals.

As you walk, you are aware of changes, there are more people, more buildings, a different style of clothes, perhaps bigger carts in the streets, more people around, a general air of bustle, but above and through it all the Angels are present.

You move forwards through time, seeing many changes taking place over the centuries: perhaps you see the first signs of the industrial revolution, the first steam vehicle, the first motor cars. You are aware that life around you is noisier, faster than at the beginning of your journey, but always the Angels are there even if they seem more elusive.

Now you have arrived in the present time: people hurry past you, there is the constant noise of traffic, the smell of petrol fumes, there are planes overhead, phones ringing, police cars wailing, blasts of pop music coming from car windows. In the rush and above all the din, it is harder to see the Angels or hear them, but when you pay close attention you realize that they are there, as they have been all along.

Gradually come back to the place where you are sitting and become aware of your body and your surroundings. Take a little time to think about the journey you have just made before you plunge back into everyday life in the present.

ONE WOMAN'S JOURNEY

Why am I writing a book about Angels? And why should I expect you to read it? The only way I can answer those questions is to describe how I was first made aware of Angels, and how that experience subsequently changed my life.

In May 1990 I was traveling home from America where I had been speaking at an aromatherapy conference and attending teachings from His Holiness the Dalai Lama. The two activities may sound rather incompatible, and certainly they could not have been more different: the conference in a plush seafront hotel, the teachings in tented accommodation at a Buddhist retreat center, but the fact that the conference organizers paid my air fare had made it possible for me to attend the teachings. Both activities are significant in the light of what happened next.

Some hours into the flight, when it was night time over the Atlantic, I had an experience that was eventually to change my life: I saw an Angel.

It was glowing gold, and appeared at first to be somewhat taller than a very tall man, but expanded until it filled the whole sky. In fact, I saw what my physical eyes could not have seen from a few thousand feet above the Atlantic, namely the Planet Earth, which was far smaller than the golden Being which was sending beams of love from its heart to the Earth.

Skeptics have suggested that I was asleep, that it was a dream, but the fact that I made a thumbnail sketch of the Angel on a page of a notebook that I had in my handbag would seem to disprove that idea. In any case, even if it had been a dream, the impact that the experience had on me was so powerful that it surpassed any dream I have ever had in my life and I attribute that to Divine influence. It would not have been the first time that an Angel manifested to a human in the form of a dream. It was fortunate that I had the paper and pens with which to make a sketch, because the vision ended with the words "Go home and paint this." This vision was all the more astonishing because I was a seriously practicing Tibetan Buddhist and the teachings were very much in my consciousness at that moment because of the time I had just spent in the presence of His Holiness the Dalai Lama. There are no Angels in Buddhism, although there are flying Beings, called dakinis. It is often thought that we see Angels - or other non-human manifestations - because we expect to, or because we want to, but nothing could have been further from my expectations, my desire or my beliefs at that time. After all, Angels are messengers of God, and Buddhism is a spiritual practice without a God. If, at that point, I had seen a dakini I would have been far less amazed!

Another commonly held idea is that Angels appear when we are in danger, and there are many well authenticated accounts of Angelic appearances around planes that were in trouble, but my homeward flight was as smooth and uneventful as any flight could be.

Once I had got over my jet-lag, I got out my brushes and tried to obey the Angel's injunction to paint him. I was very "rusty". I had not painted anything for several years because my aromatherapy work, which included teaching, committee work and writing books as well as seeing clients, had simply filled all my time. So, that first painting was not very good, and it took me two more tries before I made something with which I was even a little satisfied, though no earthly pigments can convey the light emanating from an Angel. The experience of just trying to convey it, though, was so absorbing, so joyful that I knew I would never again let my brushes sit idle for years on end.

A few weeks later, I saw a vast Angel of feminine appearance embracing the Planet Earth who appeared while I was waiting to be served in a cafe! Just as on the first occasion, I grabbed a pen and paper from my bag and made a thumbnail sketch which became a painting I called "Universal Love".

Soon, other Angels were asking to be painted. Unlike those first, dazzling encounters, they did not appear "externally", but presented themselves as powerful mental imagines when I sat to meditate. I felt bereft, as if I had lost something very precious when they no longer appeared before me in a blaze of light, but I have come to understand that those first two dazzling visions were the only way, at the that time, that the Angels could grab my attention. Once I had acknowledged their existence, they could choose quieter ways of making their presence felt.

The first of the meditation Angels appeared after a disastrous fire in the town of Totnes in Devon, U.K., to which I had recently moved. After learning that there had been several other serious fires in recent years, I asked a visiting spiritual teacher what the town needed by way of healing.

He replied that Totnes needed the healing energy of a blue Angel, and during a meditation shortly after that I was shown a blue Angel and told that that I was to paint it and then hang it in some public place in the town. When I began to paint this Angel I was given, by means of a voice in my head, very specific instructions as to how I should go about the task including methods that were quite different from the way I was used to working. This Angel, who I was subsequently told was the Archangel Raphael, hung in Totnes Natural Health Centre for quite a long time. Eventually I took it home but gave the Centre two other Angel paintings including "Universal Love", which several of the therapists working there say brings an extra healing quality to the room in which it hangs.

It would take too long to detail all the Angels that I have painted since, and the many different ways in which they have made themselves known to me which have included dreams, meditation experiences and something I call "doodle Angels" when I find myself spontaneously drawing while I am thinking of something entirely different - a shopping list, for example - Angels do have a wonderful sense of humor! I imagine them saying "Quick, she's got a pen in her hand. Show her what you want her to paint next while you've got the opportunity". Most of these doodles eventually get made into full-scale paintings.

Only once, some six years after that first encounter, did I see an Angel again "externally": she was dancing in the hallway of a house I had just bought and I painted a fresco of her on the wall just where I had seen her. I was told by a clairvoyant friend that the Angel was there to protect not only my house, but the whole of the hillside on which it stood. Some years later, when I no longer lived there, the area was threatened with overdevelopment, including building over a green open space and a fierce planning battle ensued. Eventually, the local residents won, and a greatly modified scheme emerged, in which the open space and an ancient healing well were preserved. To my surprise, a former neighbor, who had been very active in opposing the original plans stopped me in the street to say that she felt the energy of my Angel had been a major factor in their success. Until that moment, I had had no idea she had any belief or even any interest in Angels.

Of course, the paintings did not happen in a vacuum: every area of my life was changed, some subtly, some more obviously, as I believe any life must change when the Angels become part of it.

One major change was my name. A few months after my first angelic encounter, I attended a workshop given by Solara, an American teacher who had much wisdom concerning Angels to share. During the workshop there was a period of silent meditation during which she invited us to be open to hearing our soul name or angelic name, and the name that I heard was "Ishvara". This felt so right, that I adopted it straight away, initially in dealing with several close friends who had been at the workshop with me and had also had new names revealed to them. About a year later, one of those friends phoned me to say that she had found the name Ishvara in a yoga book, with a translator's note explaining what it meant. Now, until then I had no idea that the name had a meaning, but when she explained that the word was Sanskrit and translated, roughly, as "One who is able to create" it felt like a wonderful gift, a real blessing for somebody who wished to do more and more creative work and soon after that, I changed my name legally.

The desire to spend more and more time painting led me to cut down on my involvement with the world of aromatherapy. I gave up my committee work, engaged extra tutors to take on some of my duties in the training school and began to plan my eventual retirement from the school. None of this happened overnight, of course and not all of it was easy. At the point when I saw the Angel during my transatlantic flight I had just had my first taste of being treated as a celebrity a moderately big fish in a very small pond! My first book had recently been published and I had a handbag full of invitations from people I had met at the conference to go back to the United States and lecture here, teach there, give a series of workshops somewhere else. It was very tempting but somehow the Angels called louder. Nowadays, if I give a workshop or a talk, it will be about Angels, not essential oils.

My earliest ambition was to be a painter, though when I was practicing and teaching aromatherapy I felt that I was being of service to my fellow-humans but in a reading with a very special person who channeled the Archangel Gabriel I was told to let it go, because I had taught plenty of other people to do it, and do it well. Through obeying the Angels I received the precious gift of being able to follow my original dream.

But, far more important than anything affecting my career, I began to question my beliefs. For a long time I described myself as "an odd kind of Buddhist who paints Angels!" and was very uncomfortable with some of the language associated with Angels, which felt too "churchy" to me but I gradually came to accept that if Angels are messengers of God and I had experienced over and over again proof that Angels existed, then I had to accept that God existed too. The messenger could not exist without the originator of the message.

This did not mean that I abandoned everything I had learnt in the years that I had followed the Buddhist path: many of the teachings are profound truths that are common to all religions and spiritual paths. Buddhist ethics are still at the core of the way I try to live from day to day and I am full of gratitude to the teachers who instilled in me the habit of regular meditation. Rather than abandon everything I had been taught, I found that my old belief system simply expanded to embrace the wonderful fact that Angels exist and that the God who they serve exists.

So, that is how I come to be writing this book. I hope that I can share with you some of the wonderful discoveries I made along the way and that both you and I will be blessed by many more in the future.

THE NATURE OF ANGELS

What is an Angel? What do you think of when you see or hear that word? What are they made of? What is the purpose of their existence?

What is their true nature?

Some of these questions are easier to answer than others, or at least seem so initially. For example, people who agree about the existence of Angels may have many different interpretations of what that means, depending on each person's beliefs and the culture in which they have grown up.

What is the purpose of Angels? Why do they exist at all? An answer that encompasses every kind of Angel might be: to act as a bridge between humanity and the Divine.

The word "Angel" comes from the Greek "angelos" meaning a messenger or intermediary. Angelos is itself a translation of the Hebrew "mal'akh" which has come to have the same meaning although the literal translation means "the shadow side of God" referring to the belief that humans cannot look directly at the Divine because the Light would be too intense for us to bear. Angels stand between us and the Source and filter that Light.

The metaphor of an electrical transformer has often been used to describe this function, and it is an apt one. The majesty, the light and the power of the Divine is such that mortals could not experience it directly, just as we cannot tap into the electrical grid without being killed. Thanks to transformers we are able to reap the benefits of electric power in our daily lives and through the mediation of the Angels we are able to glimpse something of the Divine power and be blessed by it every day. The ways in which Angels do this are many and various and there are different kinds of Angels with specific functions, which we look at more in the chapter about Angel Families.

We tend to think of Angels as gentle, benevolent creatures, but some of them can be too awesome, too powerful for us to contemplate. The Kerubim and Seraphim, for example are beyond human imagining, so close to the Divine, so powerful that we could no more look upon them than we can look upon God. We need still further "transformers", the Archangels and Angels who act as intermediaries to transmit to us as much of their majesty as we can bear.

And who can be touched by Angelic energy without having their life transformed?

But it is as messengers of the Divine that they interact most often with humanity. Scripture and history are full of accounts of Angels bringing messages to us on Earth, and this continues to the present day. It is important to remember that they are messengers *of the Divine*. They are not autonomous Beings, they are ultimately responsible to God, the Divine, the Source, or whatever name is most meaningful to you.

What are Angels made of? Many people think that they are made of light, and certainly the manner in which they often manifest would seem to confirm this. People at the present day as well as in scripture and other writings have reported being dazzled, even temporarily blinded, by the light pouring from the Angels they have encountered - and this is despite the fact that, as we have seen above, they shelter us from the Divine Light which we could not bear.

Describing Angels as Beings of Light does seem very valid and another confirmation of this theory comes from many of the names that have been given to Angels: The Shining Ones, for example. In fact the syllable "-el" in which most Angel's names end, is often translated as "shining" although another meaning is "Divine" and Angels are both.

We can also consider the physical properties of light, especially the speed at which it travels. Compare that with the instantaneous manner in which Angels can manifest, and to speak of them moving "at the speed of light" makes a lot of sense. Life on Earth would be impossible without light. Can we bear to imagine what it would be like without Angels?

Another theory is that Angels are made of energy and this too is very persuasive. We might think of Angels as an extension of the Divine energy that permeates the whole of creation, the energy, in fact, that brought about Creation.

St. Thomas Aquinas described Angels as made of "pure intellect" - perhaps not a term we in the twenty-first century would associate with Angels. If, though, we remember that he was writing in Latin and that various translations of his words are possible, it can be taken as meaning that they are not in any way physical Beings.

But, when Angels manifest to us on Earth, do they then take on a physical form? Again, opinions vary a great deal. My own feeling is that they can and do when the situation requires it. Certainly, some of the Angelic encounters that have been reported, both in the scriptures and by people who have been blessed by meetings with Angels in our own time, suggest solidity and a tangible physical presence. In Genesis (Ch.32) we learn that when Jacob wrestled with an Angel it was a tough fight - the Angel dislocated Jacob's hip joint. Now, our modern understanding of energy tells us that could be done without the exertion of physical force, but also in Genesis (Ch. 6) we are told that Angels cohabited with human women and had children with them which is about as physical as you can get.

Equally, other people report experiences of glowing lights, subtle voices, impressions of a holy presence that are not indicative of a physical visitation. I believe that all are equally valid, that Angels can choose the most appropriate way to manifest. If a physical presence is needed in a particular situation, the Angel will manifest in physical form. If a more subtle manifestation would be better suited to the person or the situation, the Angel will choose whatever means are best to make its presence known.

Milton expressed this beautifully:

For spirits when they please,
Can either sex assume, or both; so soft
And uncompounded is their essence pure,
Not tied or manacled with joint or limb,
Nor founded on the brittle strength of bones,
Like cumbrous flesh; but in what shape they choose
Can execute their aery purposes.

Are Angels eternal? The most widely-accepted belief is that they are, that they have existed from the first moments of Creation, and will exist until the end of time. What they are not are human beings who have passed on, though there are a few notable exceptions such as the prophet Enoch who was "taken up by God", as related in the fifth chapter of Genesis, and transformed into the mightiest of all Archangels: Metatron.

I know that for some people it is comforting to believe that somebody they once loved is now an Angel who watches over them but that would deny the eternal nature of Angels. I am sure that our loved ones do indeed watch over us, but that does not make them Angels. Angels belong to a different order of creation from humanity.

That is their purpose and for this we rejoice.

WHAT DO ANGELS LOOK LIKE?

The function of the wing is to take what is heavy and raise it
up into the region above,
where the gods dwell.

PLATO.

What does an Angel look like?

Most of us have a fairly clear idea of the answer to that question -
but my idea of an Angel may not be the same as yours and neither of
our concepts are likely to be the same as that of an early Israelite! We

are unlikely to envisage a creature with seventy-two wings and a body made of fire and even less likely to think of "a wheel within a wheel" which is how Ezekiel described the Ophanim. The Seraphim, with three pairs of wings are probably more familiar, for they do find their way into European art.

If you live in a Western culture, it is likely that you envisage an Angel as a human-like form though often much taller than any human being, possibly of very great beauty, and with wings. People from other cultures and at other times in history may have very different images of spiritual messengers, which are every bit as valid for them as the classical image of the Angel is for us.

Because I am a painter I find it impossible to write about Angels, or even to think about them, without visual images arising. But for most of us, painters and non-painters alike, our concept of Angels is, inevitably, influenced by the way they have been depicted by artists. Peter Lamborn Wilson in his book "Angels" writes:

> *"The image of the Angel...emerges from a creative interplay between traditional canons - based on Scripture - and personal vision. To say that a visionary sees what Scripture and sacred art have prepared him to see is not to accuse him of inauthenticity: vision is real, but it is also influenced by culture. In the resonances created by this paradox, the Angel unveils itself."*

But I have met many people whose experience of Angels does not seem to be colored by the traditional canon; heavenly Beings have appeared to them as a column of light, dancing lights, a cloud, a beautiful (wingless) adolescent or an old man. It seems that we are less influenced now by the traditional image of Angels - perhaps because more people are becoming aware of them independently of scripture or classical art.

Artists, too, are finding different modes of expression. During the Middle Ages and the Renaissance quite rigid conventions were established as to the proper style and color of various Archangel's robes and the attributes they carried, and artists observed these right through to Victorian times, but contemporary painters feel free to depict Angels in whatever color seems right to them and any style of clothing, including present-day dress. In recent years artists have depicted Angels' wings as flames, or as rays of light, as an extension of the Angel's aura or energy field. Some are making Angels with no wings at all, and yet there is a quality in the image that tells us at once that it is an Angel.

I recall seeing for the first time a photograph of Anthony Gormley's "Angel of the North" and being really shocked by it by its airplane-type wings, though subsequently it has become one of my best-loved sculptures.

Then I reflected that for a thousand years and more painters and sculptors have given their Angels bird-like wings *because they were the only kind of wing they knew* but here we had a twentieth century sculptor using a genuinely twentieth century metaphor.

For I believe that the wings given to Angels in art of all kinds *are* a metaphor; they are way of expressing visually the fact that Angels can move between the realms of Spirit and the physical world and that they can manifest instantaneously in any place. This is not exclusive to Christian art: every civilization that became aware of a dimension beyond the physical, human plane has envisaged some form of Being that can move between the different planes of existence and most of these were and, in many cases still are, depicted as winged. Perhaps observing birds that soared until they were lost to sight first gave rise to the idea of a winged Being that could go where humans could not?

The Greeks, for example, used wings to denote Beings who could move between Olympus and Earth, and in the case of Hermes, the Messenger of the Gods, the Underworld too. They also used physical beauty to suggest spiritual beauty - what else could an artist using earthy materials and earthly models do?

The Council of Nicea in 787 A.D. decreed that it was lawful to depict Angels and the earliest Christian artists followed Graeco-Roman models, especially in their sculpture. Statues of Hermes, Eros or Nike the Winged Victory look remarkably like Angels as we mostly imagine them today.

But the Greeks were not the first or the only civilization to envisage winged Beings who acted as intermediaries between humanity and the gods. The Sumerians believed in Guardian spirits called lamassu, whose job was to protect the individual from evil and carry their prayers to the gods - in other words, very like our Guardian Angels. The earliest images of lamassu show winged bulls with human heads, but by the latter part of the Sumerian epoch they had evolved into human figures with wings.

In ancient Persia, the Zoroastrian religion incorporated a host of Angels called yazatas and six divine spirits called Amesha Spentas, whose role was virtually identical to that of the seven Archangels surrounding the Divine in the Judeo-Christian tradition. The Egyptian pantheon included a number of winged Beings - Isis is sometimes shown with wings, as is the hawk-god Horus and others at different times and different places.

Pre-Columbian sacred art from South America shows winged

messengers dating from long before the conquistadors.

At the present time, Hindus have Devas and winged maidens called Apsaras while Buddhist tradition includes the Dakinis who are not shown as winged, but who can rise spontaneously into the clouds. Dakinis may sometimes be seductive women and at other times fearsome apparitions with necklaces of skulls. Although they are not winged, the bodhisatvas of Buddhist tradition have perhaps more in common with our concept of Angels, because they are compassionate and concerned with the spiritual progress of mankind.

Islamic lore is full of Angels and Archangels who are virtually exact parallels with the familiar Angels of Western tradition, and many more besides.

Another source of ideas about the appearance of Angels has been the experience of visionaries. Inspired souls from Hildegard of Bingen to Teresa of Avila described their experiences and writers, painters, sculptors, the makers of illuminated manuscripts set them down for us all to see. In some cases, it was the painter or sculptor him- or herself who was a visionary, and set down in paint or stone what he or she had experienced at first hand and this is still happening at the present time. Some of the pictures of Angels that are emerging now bear little resemblance to traditional ideas but are totally convincing because they represent honestly the personal experience of the person who painted them.

The traditional, Western concept of an Angel, which stems mainly from mediaeval and renaissance art, does embody certain truths. For example, the Angels familiar to us from the work of Fra Angelico or Botticelli tend to be androgynous in appearance, and I believe that this reflects a profound truth: namely that Angels are neither male nor female, but can choose to appear to us in the guise of whichever sex is most appropriate to the situation in which they manifest.

Have we made Angels in our own image?

I like to think that, in their infinite love and compassion for us, they choose to show themselves in the form to which we can relate most fully.

ANGEL FAMILIES AND ANGEL WORK

Have you ever considered how orderly the Universe is? How everything has its place, its time and its purpose? How nothing is haphazard?

How night follows day, Spring follows Winter, the Moon waxes and wanes and the tides move with her? How, when you plant an acorn it grows into an oak, not into a beech or an ash? How, when a tiger gives birth to cubs they will be striped, not spotted? How certain plants and animals are perfectly adapted to live in specific climates and surroundings, so that each has its special place?

This orderliness pervades the Universe from the greatest galaxy to the smallest particle. The planets keep their orbits, the stars appear in their accustomed places and at the other end of the scale, every atom, every cell in our bodies, has its own precise design. It is probably true to say that, tragically, where order is not found, this is because of human intervention.

I believe that the Angels are to a large degree responsible for maintaining this wonderful order in the Universe and that one of the reasons they are manifesting on Earth with ever increasing frequency at the present time may be to help us restore natural order to our Planet.

So it should come as no surprise that there is order among the Angels.

Just as plants and animals, stars and planets have their allotted places within a greater design, Angels have theirs too, and their own specific "work" to do.

For over a thousand years, scholars and mystics have sought to describe how Angels are organized into various orders or "families". The most widely accepted account of the Angelic orders is that written down in the 6th century by a mystic known as Dionysius the Ariopagite. He described how Angels are organized into nine Orders, which are further divided into three groups of three. There are other theories regarding the Angelic orders, as well as later variations on Dionysius' scheme but the majority of them agree that there are 9 orders of Angels. I find Dionysius' description the clearest, the one that rings true for me and I feel that it certainly still has value for us at the present day. I suspect this is because he drew directly on his own mystical experiences and those of a number of mystics before him and, given the direct and personal nature of mystical experience, it is better able to describe the nature of the Angelic realms than any amount of theorizing.

The nine groups of Angels are sometimes referred to as Angel "choirs" which can be a little misleading, given our understanding of the word as meaning a group of singers. Angels do, indeed, sing and for some of them, that is their continual occupation and their sole purpose, but other Angels have many and varied responsibilities. Another expression often used in older or more traditional literature is Angel hierarchies. Unfortunately, the word has gathered unwelcome connotations, suggesting rigidity, power struggles, authority and subservience, and nothing could be further from the Angelic truth. So,

I propose to use the term "Angel families".

The first group of three families are the Seraphim, the Kerubim and the Ophanim. These are the Angels who are spend their whole existence close to the Divine.

The Seraphim could most truly be called a choir of Angels, for they spend eternity in the contemplation of the Divine and praising God continuously, chanting "Holy, holy, holy" as they endlessly circle the Creator's throne. They glory in the beauty of the Divine. Isaiah called them "burning" or "fiery ones" - perhaps because the light that emanates from them is intense beyond our imagining, or maybe as a way of describing the burning passion with which they praise God and the equal passion with which they infuse the lower orders of Angels.

Next come the Kerubim. I have chosen to use this spelling rather than the alternative, Cherubim, because the latter is too easily identified with the little fat, winged babies who turn up on Christmas cards and calendars!

No image could be more misleading: the Kerubim are Beings of such might and power that we cannot even begin to imagine what they might look like. The name Kerubim means "fullness of knowledge" and their work is to transmit the wisdom and the energy of the Divine to the Angelic orders beneath them.

Think of an electrical transformer making the power in the national grid accessible to us for everyday uses. Without the transformer we would be burnt up.

The third family in this group are the Ophanim, who are sometimes called Thrones, though the name is also sometimes translated as Wheels. Their work is to lift our souls up towards the Divine. We cannot conceive of their appearance, though Ezekiel said they were "as a wheel in the middle of a wheel" - certainly not anything resembling a body. Perhaps they are pure spirit? We cannot know what they look like. They are probably formless, at least in terms that we, as humans can understand, pure spirit, pure energy.

The same, I think is probably true of the Seraphim and Kerubim, though mediaeval artists have traditionally portrayed the Seraphim as having three pairs of red wings, but I suspect this is an attempt to convey the idea of fieriness. Kerubim were often shown with a single pair of blue wings.

This first, highest group of Angels may seem very remote from us and our daily lives, but as well as empowering the other Angelic orders, they act as shining examples that we may emulate to the best of our human ability. Few of us, other than the members of some closed monastic orders, can devote our lives to praise and contemplation, but we can all try to make space in our lives for quiet time when we are open to Spirit. We can pause to notice beauty wherever it occurs, glory in it and give thanks for it.

The second group of Angelic families are the Dominions, Powers and Virtues. The Angels of these families are responsible for receiving Light or energy from those in the first group of families, and transmitting it to those in the third group and they do this in a variety of ways.

It is harder to describe in human terms what the functions of this second group of Angels are. It is, perhaps, useful to remember the analogy with an electric transformer, for they constantly receive energy from the first group of Angelic families and transmit them to the third group. They act as receptors and transmitters of praise, awe and wisdom and inspire those beneath them.

The Angels who interact directly with humanity belong to the third group of families: the Principalities, Archangels and Angels. When we have an Angelic experience, or read or hear of others doing so, it is with a member of one of these families.

The Principalities are traditionally described as Angels concerned with the fate of individual nations, though some believe that their role is more to do with the maintenance of moral or spiritual principles on Earth. I must say that I incline to the latter view, for I find it hard to believe that dividing the people of this Planet into separate nations is a matter in which Angels are, or ever have been, involved. Rather, if we consider how nationalism, racism and other forms of division have served to promote strife and wars throughout the ages, we might suspect that all these horrors are the result of humanity distancing itself from the Divine. Surely the greatest desire of the Principalities is to guide the nations of the Earth towards peace and harmony if only world leaders would heed them. Conversely, it may be that even though the present state of the world may seem to our human minds to be so terrible, this is part of the Divine plan.

But the Principalities are also Angels of place: they are the protectors of the land regardless of who lives upon it and in the course of human history any given parcel of Earth will have seen many waves of different inhabitants. The Principalities, throughout our history and long before it, have looked after the rocks and rivers, the very soil itself, of the lands of which they are protectors.

The Archangels, who are the second family in this group, are the most powerful of those who manifest on Earth. Beings of great might, power and beauty, they have been present at pivotal events in humanity's history. The role of the four great Archangels: Gabriel, Michael, Raphael, and Uriel, at this moment in history is so important that I have devoted a separate section of this book to them.

Finally, we come to the Angels, and of all the members of this great company, these are the Beings who have always had the most intimate connection with humanity, and indeed with everything on Earth, for included in this family are the Devas, elementals or nature spirits, who care for the mineral, plant and animal kingdoms. They are under the direct command of the Archangels and if we invoke the aid of one of the great Archangels it may well be that the help we need will come through the intervention of an Angel carrying out the Archangel's instructions.

These are the Angels with whom we can commune on a daily basis, our guides and personal Guardians. Nothing is too small to merit their involvement, nothing is to great for them to deal with. It is only our own imperfections that limit the extent to which we can work with them. They wish for nothing more than to work with us to the fullest possible degree, and will do everything in their power to help us towards that end.

We need only to ask.

Personal, Guardian Angels are a very important part of this group, so special that we will consider them in more detail in the next chapter.

GUARDIAN ANGELS

Apart from the Angels in the school nativity play, the idea of a personal Guardian is often our earliest introduction to the idea of Angelic Beings. Perhaps we are taught about them at school or Sunday school or a parent uses the idea of a benevolent watcher to calm a sleepless child.

Sadly, though, so many of us forget about our Guardian as we grow older. The pressure of study and examinations, teenage rejection of parental values, all the stresses of growing up: work, money, relationships, maybe becoming parents, can push thoughts about Angels into some very dim compartment at the back of the mind. Sadly, because awareness of an ever-present Angel to guide us through life could make all those issues so much easier to deal with.

But even if we forget our Guardians they do not forget us.

They are with us every moment of our life on Earth, whether we are aware of it or not, but nothing gives these Angels greater delight than to communicate and work with us consciously. Some who believe that we live more than one life on this Earth consider that the same Guardian is with us throughout each lifetime, though others believe that we are given a new Guardian at each incarnation, because the conditions of each lifetime are different. What is sure it that our Guardians are with us from before birth until the end of our Earthly life. This is true even if we ignore them, even if we reject the idea of Angels altogether. How much more fruitful, though, if we make our relationship with our Guardian a two-way process.

It helps to make a habit of talking to your personal Angel, just as you would to a friend. Share your worries and doubts and remember to listen for your Angel's answers. Ask for guidance when you have to make important decisions. Ask for help when life is tough. Nothing is too big or too small.

If it matters to you, then it matters to your Guardian. If you need the help of a different Angel or Archangel your Guardian will make sure that your needs are known.

We should not, though, fall into the habit of regarding our Guardian Angel as a kind of personal assistant! There is a fairly widespread notion that it is permissible to ask your Angel to keep a parking space free for you, or make sure all the traffic lights are green when you are in a hurry, but this is abusing the kindness of your Guardian, unless there is a genuine need. For example, Trish needed to get a sick child to hospital as quickly as possible. The G.P. had examined the little boy and rung for an ambulance, but was told there was none available for 40 minutes, so it was much quicker for Trish to take him in her own car. On that occasion it felt perfectly right to ask for help with traffic lights. She was able to drive to the hospital in record time, there was a parking space right near the hospital entrance and the little boy was in the operating theatre very speedily, for which she thanked both his Guardian and her own.

It can make it easier to have such conversations if you know your Guardian's name and one way to find out is to ask to be told it before you go to sleep. You may hear a name, or have a dream in which the name is mentioned, or a name might plant itself in your head. You may possibly need to ask several times before you become aware of the answer. Don't be put off if what you are told does not sound like a typical Angel's name: your Guardian may be called something as plain as Tom or Mary, or something very complicated indeed as is illustrated in the following story from a man called Joe.

Joe believes in God and Angels, but not in any formal religion. He had read that asking before going to sleep was a way to discover the name of one's Guardian and decided to try it. At first he heard nothing but he persevered and eventually he did, indeed, hear a name, Spitzberger. Not at all convinced that this could be the name of his Guardian he decided to ask for another sign: if the lottery ticket he had bought the previous day had won him any money, he would believe the name really belonged to his Guardian. In fact, he had four numbers correct and had won a small amount of money. Joe does not believe in coincidences and from then on he has accepted that his Guardian really is called Spitzberger! A year or two later his Angel was instrumental in his recovery from cancer. Joe says, "I now have a very strong belief in Angels and the powers they have been given to help mankind."

Skeptics question the existence of Guardian Angels, pointing to tragic accidents, illnesses and other personal trauma and asking "Where was the Angel then?" but guarding us from physical harm is not the first priority of our Guardian. Our Guardians may, indeed, keep us out of danger, especially if it is not time for us to die - and there are many, well-attested examples of miraculous escapes that could only be attributed to Angelic intervention - but their true role is to guard us from spiritual harm. It grieves our Guardians when we stray from the spiritual path, and they strive, above all, to keep us from doing so. If we are aware of their constant presence, and endeavor to work consciously with them, it becomes a continual joy to live our lives in harmony with the highest spiritual truths.

A MEDITATION TO MEET YOUR GUARDIAN ANGEL

This is a meditation that I include in my workshops, and it has helped many people to recognize their personal Angels.

Take a little time to be quiet and still before you begin.

Now, imagine that you are in a beautiful and quiet place in the country, somewhere where you feel safe and happy. What can you see? What can you hear? Can you smell anything? Can you feel the ground beneath your feet, or a little breeze against your skin? As you walk slowly in this beautiful place, you come to a lake with an island in the middle and you notice that a little boat is tethered to a small jetty nearby. You get into the boat and row out to the island, tying the boat up securely as you step ashore.

Walking towards the center of the island, you come to a clearing which has a very special atmosphere. It feels sacred, as if some higher Being is present. You sit down, or kneel on the soft grass and ask for this Being to make itself known to you. In the stillness you may hear a voice, a name, or some special words; you may see the Angel before you in whatever form it chooses to manifest for you; you may feel a presence; you may smell some delicate perfume but whichever way the Being chooses to manifest, you know that it is your personal Angel and you are filled with joy.

After a while, you become aware that the experience has faded, and you gently get up and begin to walk back to the boat, but your heart is full and you know that the memory of this special time will stay with you always. You row back across the lake, tie up the boat and begin to make your way home.

Allow yourself some time to absorb this experience before you take a few deep breaths and open your eyes. You may want to write down what you have just heard, seen or felt or some people like to draw a picture of their experience (it doesn't matter if it is not great art!).

PART TWO

ARCHANGELS IN OUR TIME

ARCHANGELS IN OUR TIME

Ye hosts Angelic by the high Archangels led,
Heavenly powers beneficent
Mighty in the Music of the Word,
Great ones entrusted with the sovereignty
Marshalling the Cherubim and flaming Seraphim,
Ye, O Michael, Prince of Heaven
And Gabriel, by whom the Word is given,
Uriel, great Archangel of the Earth.
Raphael of healing ministry to those who yet in bondage are,
Guide our footsteps as we journey onward
Into Light Eternal.

EUSEBIUS, (200 A.D.)

There are many ways we can work in partnership with the Angels, from prayer and meditation at one extreme to activism at the other - which is not to say we can't pray, meditate and take action! - and to understand how we can do this in partnership with the Angels, it may help to consider the four great Archangels and how they relate to the world we are living in now.

GABRIEL, THE HERALD OF CHANGE

Of all the Archangels, Gabriel embodies the role of messenger most fully: he is the principal messenger, the herald. More specifically, he is the Herald of Change.

Gabriel's name means "Man-God" because of all the Archangels he is thought to be the most able to take on a human-like appearance. Gabriel is gifted with this ability to manifest easily in human form because he is the most direct intermediary between humanity and the Divine.

Certainly, in biblical accounts of Angels being seen Gabriel seems to appear most often and the image of Gabriel as the Angel of the Annunciation figures in more paintings than any other Archangel and turns up in books, on calendars and cards and in the children's annual nativity play. Because of this, he is probably the most familiar of all the Archangels, a reassuring and comforting presence.

In the Islamic tradition, Gabriel is known as Jibriel (or Jibreel), and is thought to have 140 pairs of wings, signifying his ability to be in all places simultaneously. Jibriel is said to have dictated the Koran to Mohammed.

I refer to Gabriel as "he", but there are some who think Gabriel is feminine. This may be because he appears frequently in biblical narrative in connection with pregnancy and birth, most notably of course the birth of Jesus, though there are several other instances. Certainly many portrayals of Gabriel in European art appear feminine, or at least androgynous but this is not very reliable evidence as even such robust Angels as the Archangel Michael often appear quite feminine in mediaeval and renaissance paintings.

My own belief is that Angels are neither male nor female, but can choose to manifest as either, so let us say that Gabriel embodies a gentle, feminine energy. Which is not to say a weak energy! It is a driving force - you can't avoid it.

If Gabriel manifests in your life, something is bound to change. The change may be minor, or it may turn your life upside down. But change is often uncomfortable, challenging, sometimes frightening: we tend to resist it, to prefer the status quo.

We can see an example of this in the best known of all the stories involving Gabriel: the Annunciation. Mary did not initially welcome the news of her impending pregnancy with delight. Luke tells us she was "greatly troubled"- quite understandably, given all the circumstances. Imagine a teenage girl with no sexual experience, engaged to an older man, being told she is pregnant. Next, she passed through a phase of accepting her destiny and only later did she feel able to rejoice.

So what significance does this have for us, now? How many of us have resisted a "wake-up call" from the Divine, been reluctant to accept that we have a spiritual destiny? We may think "My life's just fine the way it is." or, "I'm too busy to pray, meditate, etc.," or "It's all very well to talk about retraining as a therapist, but I've got a mortgage to pay, kids to bring up." (A wise man - I wish I knew his name - once said "The spiritual is seldom convenient!")

But we do have free will. If we do not want to hear Gabriel's message we are free to turn a deaf ear, but we may never know what joy and fulfillment we sacrifice by doing so. In refusing to hear the Herald we may never reach our personal Magnificat.

And how might the Herald manifest in your life or mine? Probably not with a beating of wings and a rustle of robes! We need to be open and sensitive to the messages which may come to us through intuition, through channeling, through "coincidences", a picture, a piece of music that has some special resonance, a book that "jumps off the shelf" or draws our eye to the shop window, a chance remark we overhear and above all, through being still and receptive. When we pay attention to Gabriel's message, when we embrace change willingly, we open up our lives to magical possibilities.

In his role of messenger par excellence, Gabriel shares many characteristics with the Greek Hermes (Mercury to the Romans) who was the messenger of the Olympian gods. But Hermes had another role, which was that of the psychopompos, or guide of souls. The classical civilizations believed that Hermes/Mercury was able to move freely between the upper world of Olympus (Heaven), the Earth and the underworld: a rare attribute, and so he was able to guide the soul at death. In the Egyptian pantheon, Anubis played a similar, though not quite identical role.

Gabriel in fact shares this role with Hermes, as well as that of Divine messenger although this is far less familiar to us than the part he plays in relation to birth. If you see a depiction of Gabriel holding a palm-leaf, as opposed to the more familiar lily, he is in attendance upon a departing soul rather than one entering this world.

There is some overlap here between the roles of Gabriel and of the Archangel Azriel, and you will find some thoughts about Azriel a little further on. But whatever name we use, to be aware of the closeness of these gentlest of Archangels can be of the utmost comfort to people nearing the end of this life, and to their loved ones and carers.

A MEDITATION
WITH THE ARCHANGEL GABRIEL

Prepare yourself for meditation in your accustomed way.

Imagine that you are in a place where you feel very secure and comfortable. It may be your own home - possibly the very room in which you are meditating - or some other familiar place where you feel safe and at ease. Take in the details of the familiar surroundings.

Suddenly, an unfamiliar Being presents itself in your familiar place. You are surprised, maybe even a bit alarmed, but you recognize that this is the Archangel Gabriel, and feel reassured.

You understand that Gabriel has a message for you: it may be that you hear Gabriel's voice in your meditation, or some inner voice that seems to be within your own mind. Perhaps Gabriel hands you a written message, or tells you to be alert for signs that you will come across in the next few days.

Then, as suddenly as he arrived, Gabriel is gone.

Gradually return to the here and now - if the safe place in which you chose to be in the meditation was your own home this will probably be easier and faster than usual, but do be sure that you are fully grounded and alert.

Reflect on the message you have been given. How does it make you feel? Is it welcome and reassuring? Or are you worried or alarmed by it? Does it suggest that you have to make some changes in the way you live? Be assured that however you feel at this moment, the message and any actions that you take as a result are in accordance with your greatest spiritual good.

This is simpler than some of the meditations suggested elsewhere in this book, but I ask you to think deeply upon it, to continue thinking about it for a while, to be alert to anything you become aware of in the following few days that connects with the Archangel's message. Pay extra-special attention to anything that you read or hear, for example, to the people that you meet, the thoughts that pass through your mind, and examine any significance that they may have that connects with the Archangel's message

MICHAEL THE COMMANDER

More than any other Archangel, Michael is the Angel of Our Time.

According to some traditions, Gabriel ruled the era from just before the birth of Jesus until the late 19th century, handing authority then to Michael who rules the present era. He is the Archangel who guides us in the twenty-first century and into the "New Age".

He is *our* inspiration, *our* leader and he is here, above all, to remind us that we are spiritual Beings.

Although the literal translation of his Hebrew name means "Who is as God", the Archangel Michael is often referred to as "The Commander in Chief", "Commander of the Heavenly Host", "The Overlord" or similar titles because all the other Archangels are linked to him and take their orders from him. Michael alone receives his orders direct from the Divine Source. He was also the commander of the Angels who turned Lucifer/Satan and his followers our of heaven when they disobeyed God..

His importance is, perhaps, reflected by the fact that in many countries he is knows as Saint Michael: St. Michel in France, San Michele in Italy and so forth because he was so highly venerated, especially in the Middle Ages. But it is important to remember that he was never a "saint" in the sense of a human Being who has led a life of exemplary spirituality. He has always been, is now and for eternity will be the most powerful of the Archangels, an immortal Being.

In art, Michael is usually depicted carrying a sword, or a spear and quite often he is shown wearing armor. This, coupled with his many military-sounding titles, is puzzling for people who find it hard to reconcile such warlike imagery with the nature of a great Archangel. To understand this, we need to look beyond the surface appearances to the deeper symbolism.

Michael carries a sword in order to cut through ignorance. It is interesting to note that in this respect he resembles the bodhisatva Manjushri in Buddhist tradition, who is also shown carrying a sword for exactly the same purpose. Sometimes Michael is shown subduing (*not* killing) a dragon with either his sword or a spear, the dragon representing greed.

But what is "ignorance"? We're not talking about education or the lack of it, or about a knowledge of facts, literature, mathematics or anything like that. We are talking about spiritual ignorance, a state of not-knowing. But there are more than one kind of ignorance.

A person may be spiritually ignorant because they have never had the opportunity to discover the truth, perhaps because of lack of education, or because they live under a repressive regime that denies its people access to information. Such people are deserving of our sympathy, especially if we have the privilege of knowing what they do not know. But this kind of ignorance implies the ability to learn, to wake up to truths and people who have been deprived of the opportunity to hear spiritual truths often respond rapidly, passionately and with great joy when such truths are presented to them. For them,

Michael and the other Angels have nothing but compassion.

Michael's compassion, though, can sometimes be vigorous! It can be likened to the actions of a parent who punishes a child with the child's best interests at heart, and this is never more true than of individuals who are ignorant because they are lazy! They could get at the truth if they wanted but can't be bothered! They know - somewhere in the back of their mind - that there are books in the library, lectures and workshops that might lead them towards the life of the spirit. They might even think about enrolling in a workshop or reading one of the books, but they never quite get around to it. Or they attend the workshops, read the books, but do not apply any of the teachings to the conduct of their day-to-day lives which is arguably worse.

If we willfully ignore the knowledge that could guide us towards a more spiritual life, if we deliberately close our eyes to the evils going on around us because the knowledge is too uncomfortable, we may merit a little prod from Michael's sword!

Michael's greatest battle, though, is against the forces of greed that are corrupting the world. Think about it for a moment: wars are fought, people oppressed, populations go hungry, children die, the Earth is polluted because of greed. The lust for oil, uranium, water, land, money or power lies at the root of so much that is wrong in our world. All the wars that have been fought, and are still being fought as I write, ultimately originate from greed.

Michael moves our hearts and minds to oppose the forces of greed: if we move our savings from a High Street bank to an ethical counter-part, if we protest against abuses of human rights, if we oppose all war, if we sit down in the path of the road-builders, we are collaborating with Michael. But to be partners with the Angels and Archangels we need to do these things with compassion, to learn to forgive the abusers and despoilers - however difficult that may be.

This may sound like politicizing this great Archangel, and to some that may be objectionable, but this is not the politics of left against right, of nation against nation. It is the politics of ethics and morality and I truly believe that ethics and morality are inseparable from the spiritual life.

Although it is not one of his "official" titles, another appropriate name for the Archangel Michael could be "The Angel of Judgment". I mentioned earlier that in traditional art he is generally shown with a sword or spear, but there is an equally strong tradition of depicting him holding a pair of scales: usually with a sword in one hand and the scales in the other.

Countless mediaeval panel paintings and frescoes of the Last Judgment show Michael separating the good souls from the bad and dispatching the former to Heaven while the latter are consigned to very gruesome representations of Hell. Some of these, especially from the earlier periods, are very literal in ways that may appear to the modern eye as naive; for example, there may be a miniature, naked human, representing the soul in one cup of the scales, and a pile of books and objects representing that person's bad deeds in the other. Satan, or some smaller devil acting on his behalf may be dragging on the "evil" side of the scales to make it seem even heavier, but where we see this, we also see that Michael's sword is directed towards the devil. Even in the action of judging us, Michael is on our side.

His compassion is such that in Islamic lore he is believed to weep over the sins of the faithful.

Our perception now may be less literal, but the underlying truth remains the same. Michael's greatest joy would be not to find a single soul lacking.

This function, of weighing the soul, is something that Michael shares with the Egyptian goddess Ma'at, just as we saw earlier that he could be compared with the Buddhist Manjushri. It is no accident that we find such parallels between various religions, for certain truths supercede the differences between the many different ways in which human beings have sought to understand Spirit.

Michael demands of us that we exercise discernment in spiritual and moral matters. This might involve major decisions, such as distinguishing between true teachers and misleading gurus, but it may equally mean making moral choices in our daily lives about seemingly mundane matters such as where to shop and what to buy. Should I buy the fair-trade coffee even though it costs more? Should I get my vegetables from the supermarket or the local greengrocer? Can I shut my mind to the fact that a £3.99 pair of jeans could not possibly have been made without exploiting women and children in a Third World sweatshop? Spiritual practice does not end at the High Street!

Some decisions may be far more demanding and far-reaching in their effect on our lives. For example, James worked for an old, well-established company and earned a very good salary, he enjoyed his job, knew with neither false modesty or undue pride that he was good at it and looked forward to promotion, possibly to a major position in time. Then the company was taken over by a larger, multi-national corporation and James gradually became aware that the business ethics of his new bosses was, at the very least, questionable. The more he learnt of their dealings the more uncomfortable he felt about remaining in the company. But, he had to consider the impact that resigning might have on his wife and their three children. Could he expect them to accept a lower standard of living if he took a substantial drop in salary and forfeited the likelihood of promotion?

This is the sort of dilemma in which calling upon the Archangel Michael for guidance can be profoundly helpful.

In the end James did resign, with his wife's full understanding and consent. He took a post with an ethically-aware company, and although the starting salary was lower and the prospects of promotion perhaps slower he was happier and his family were undoubtedly the better for having a happy father and husband rather than one who was stressed by ignoring the promptings of his conscience.

Archangel Michael also asks us to be discerning in our choice of friends and companions as well as our business associates. We may have to ask ourselves whether or not a particular friendship serves our spiritual development. It may even be that we have to subject a marriage or partnership to such scrutiny, painful though that may be. It often happens that as we mature in our spiritual development, old friendships no longer feel appropriate and gradually fade without any great trauma on either side.

But it can be that old friends who do not share our path feel hurt by what seems to them a distancing and divergence of interests. How can we deal with such situations without causing pain? Again, I think that to meditate or pray for guidance can be the best thing to do. The meditation suggested at the end of this chapter might be appropriate.

Another area where Michael's power of judgment may come into play is in conflict resolution. Despite his military-sounding titles, his sword and spear and the manner in which he has traditionally been depicted, Michael - like all the Angels and Archangels - desires peace on Earth. In the troubled times that we are living through, we can and we must call upon Michael to inspire wise judgment in world leaders so that war is no longer seen as a solution to every dispute.

In other words, Michael is not detached from the affairs of the modern world, he is close to us and concerned for our spiritual well-being. He cherish us, and our Planet, with the tenderness of a loving parent and the passion of a lover.

A MEDITATION
WITH THE ARCHANGEL MICHAEL

As always, make sure that you are comfortably seated and spend as much time as you need quietening your mind.

Now, with your eyes closed, imagine that you are standing in front of a large and imposing building. There is a steep flight of steps leading up to it and you climb them and arrive at a heavy door with an Angel standing guard on either side. They usher you inside and you find yourself in a large hall.

In front of you stands a huge, winged figure holding a sword in one hand and a pair of scales in the other: the Archangel Michael. At first you feel quite overawed, but he beckons to you gently and leads you to a circular table where some others are already seated. You realize that some of them are Angels while others are human like yourself.

The Archangel then puts a difficult moral question to the group gathered round the table, and requests that you discuss it and arrive at a decision.

This is far from easy, and you spend some time considering every aspect of the problem with your Angelic and human companions. At last you reach a conclusion, and inform the Archangel of it. He agrees that your decision is wise and thanks you before you leave his presence.

Take a little time to return fully to the here and now, and a little more to think about the moral problem that Michael asked you to consider.

Does it have any bearing on your everyday life? Would you have reached the same conclusion if you had considered it on your own?

This meditation could be valuable at times when you have to reach a difficult moral decision in real life. In that event, form a clear question in your mind before you sit to meditate, and imagine that this is the problem that Michael places before yourself and the Angels.

RAPHAEL THE HEALER

Raphael is another Archangel who embodies a feminine energy although he has a masculine name. The most usual translation of that name is "Divine Healer" though perhaps a more beautiful translation is "The Shining One Who Heals". The Hebrew syllable rapha translates as "doctor", "surgeon" or "healer", to which is added the suffix "el" meaning "shining" or "divine" that we find in almost all Angelic names.

When Jacob wrestled with an Angel, it was Raphael who healed his injured thigh.

Raphael brings with him healing of all kinds: for the body, mind and spirit but also for relationships, for organizations and situations and for the Earth itself, in partnership with Uriel.

Raphael is also the protector of travelers, and this, as well as his role in healing both physical and psychological ills, is illustrated in the best-known story about him, the chronicle of Tobias and the Angel, told in the apocryphal Book of Tobit. Tobit, in his latter years, has become blind and wishes only for death. Intending to put his afairs in order, he sends his son Tobias on a long journey to collect some money held on his behalf by a distant relative. He insists though, that Tobias finds a trusty travelling companion for the hazardous journey and at a hiring fair Tobias finds such a person.

During the journey, his companion helps Tobias catch a fish that will restore his father's sight. At the end of the journey the fellow-traveler also "casts out demons" from Sara, a distant cousin of Tobias with whom the young man has fallen in love, so that he is able to marry her - nowadays, we might call this healing her neuroses. After they have returned safely home, his traveling companion then shows Tobias how to cure his father's blindness with the gall of the fish, and only then does he reveal his identity as the Archangel Raphael.

A present-day story concerning travel was told to me by Angela who, with her husband and two friends, went to Paris for a short break. It was the first time Angela and her husband had been on holiday without their children who were being looked after by their grandparents. On the day they were due to fly home they arrived at Charles de Gaulle airport and found it strikebound. They were told it would be at least four days before they might get a flight home. They investigated other ways of getting home: hiring a car, trying to get to a different airport, etc., but none seemed possible.

While the two husbands tried to think of a solution, Angela and her friend Margaret prayed. Going back to their husbands, they found them talking to an unusually tall and powerfully built man who said he could help them get home, but they must hurry because a bus would be leaving soon. The itinerary that he proposed involved bus, train, Eurostar, the London Underground and then another train to Liverpool. At every change, he appeared and guided them on to the next stage, guiding them through crowds and on to the correct platform. When there was a delay he warned them of it before it was announced and when a huge queue looked like making them miss a train, he ushered them to the front of it and spoke to a ticket collector who opened the barrier, let them through and shut the barrier again immediately. Only when they were about to board the Liverpool-bound train on the final stage of the journey and he told them they would be fine now, did they ask his name as they said goodbye. He replied that he was Dave. Dave Snow. On that last train home, Margaret realized that Dave Snow was an anagram of "Saved Now" and about eighteen months later, Angela learned during a meditation that Dave was in fact the name of her personal Guardian.

Several factors mark this experience as a genuine Angel encounter: first, the stranger's unusual height, next that he knew every train time, every connection, the departure platform and so forth at each step of the way and on five different systems, which it is extremely unlikely one human would know. Then the fact that the four adults followed him implicitly, as Angela put it "like children following their teacher on an outing", and finally, that he revealed his name only as he was leaving them which is a feature of so many Angelic encounters. I think it is safe to say that "Dave" is one of Raphael's host of helpers.

As the Divine Healer, Raphael brings harmony where there is conflict and just as Uriel overlights all Nature Angels and spirits, so Raphael guides all healing Angels, for whenever healing takes place, Angels are present.

Whatever your personal concept of Angels, I believe that statement holds true.

If you conceive of Angels as vortexes of benevolent energy, it is easy to see how that energy can be involved in healing. If you hold the traditional view that Angels are messengers of the Divine, then we can see that they are a way of transmitting Divine healing energy to where it is needed. If you are of the school of thought that says Angels are something within ourselves, our higher consciousness perhaps, then it is perfectly possible that shifting something in our consciousness can also bring about healing.

I have spoken with many therapists, healers and their clients who have seen, heard or otherwise been aware of Angelic presences during sessions.

Non-professional people, too, often experience the presence of Angels if they pray or meditate for a loved friend or relative. When somebody very close to me underwent major, life-saving surgery I saw during meditation a great Angel standing behind the surgeon and since then I have learnt that this is a frequent image in such situations.

Raphael and the Angels that work with him assist in healing, whether the healer or the person seeking help are aware of it or not, but they can intervene far more powerfully if we actively invoke their help. The Angels respect our free will, so when we consciously ask for their help, they are free to work at their most powerful. Prayer, meditation or just a simple request also makes us more open and receptive to the help they can bring.

If you are a healer, doctor, nurse, physical therapist, psycho-therapist, counselor or mediator you will find your work greatly enhanced if you ask the Archangel Raphael for his presence and guidance.

There may already be a specific Angel who works with and through you, in which case you can ask for that Angel to be with you throughout the session, or you may ask to be assisted by whichever Angel is most appropriate for the person who is in need of help. Sometimes more than one Angel will be present during healing - whole crowds of them at times! - but remember that Raphael overlights and guides them all.

Given the terrible and distressing things that have happened, and continue to happen all over the world, it is most appropriate to ask Raphael to send healing to all those affected by such events. Not only to the injured children, the bereaved parents, the tortured prisoners, but also to the people in positions of power, that they be healed of their pride and folly so that such things never happen again.

Raphael and his Angels do not confine their compassion and healing to human beings. There are many instances of animals healed by Angelic intervention and I am sure that if we ask for healing for a threatened forest or a polluted lake, for example, our pleas will be heard, so we can all remember to ask Raphael, as well as Uriel, to help us heal our Planet.

As well as healing physical ills, Raphael heals relationships. In the story of Tobias quoted above, the Archangel "casts out demons" from Sara so that Tobias can marry her. Relationship conflicts are the source of so much unhappiness, not only for the two people involved but often for their families as well, and sometimes with wider repercussions when a partner has been unfaithful. It is appropriate to call on Raphael if your relationship is in trouble, or if you are concerned for a couple who are in strife, also if you work as a counselor or mediator in such situations.

A MEDITATION
WITH THE ARCHANGEL RAPHAEL

Once you have settled yourself comfortably and quietened your breath, imagine that you are in a place where there is great suffering. You can hear the moans of the dying, the screams of injured people, the tears of distraught relatives. You feel strongly drawn to help in some way, but you do not know how and you feel powerless until you think of calling on the Angels for help.

Suddenly, it is as if a veil is lifted and you become aware that a great Archangel is present. His outspread wings span the whole space and a huge crowd of Angels follow in his train. You realize that it is Raphael and his multitude of healing helpers.

You watch as they move among the sick and the injured bringing peace and healing. The cries and screams diminish until a great peace fills the place and a glowing pink light bathes everything and everybody in sight.

The visions fades, but you know that although you can no longer see them, the Angels of healing are always within reach and respond at once to our cries for help.

As always, take some time to return to earthly reality, but keep this vision and the knowledge it has given you in your heart.

It would be appropriate to practice this meditation when you are in need of healing or wish to ask for healing for others.

URIEL THE GUARDIAN OF EARTH

Glory be to God for dappled things -
For skies of couple-colour as a brindled cow;
For rose-moles all in stipple upon trout that swim;
Fresh-firecoal chestnut-falls; finches' wings;
Landscape plotted and pieced - fold, fallow, and plough;
And all trades, their gear and tackle and trim.
All things counter, original, spare, strange;
Whatever is fickle, freckled (who knows how?)
With swift, slow; sweet, sour; adazzle, dim, He fathers-forth
whose beauty is past change:
Praise him.

GERARD MANLEY HOPKINS

If Gabriel is the most familiar of the four great Archangels, Uriel is perhaps the least. He is not mentioned by name in the Bible and what we know of him comes mainly from the apocrypha. He is less often depicted in art or written about than Gabriel or Michael, for example. And yet he is a Being of tremendous importance to everyone living on Planet Earth, especially at this time.

The name Uriel is usually translated as "Regent of the Sun", or sometimes as "Flame of God". He regulates the daily passage of the Sun across our sky which creates day and night, summer and winter and without the Sun, the great flame at the center of our Solar system, life on Earth would not be possible. Uriel's chief work is to take care of the Planet Earth.

Whatever harms Planet Earth causes deep distress to Uriel. Can you imagine how Uriel suffers because of deforestation, the disappearance of plant and animal species, the pollution of air and water, the breakdown of the ozone layer and the industrial rape of the Earth?

All nature spirits, plant devas, elementals, even the tiny ones that we call fairies, are under the guidance of Uriel. They are the Guardians of the trees, plants, rivers and oceans, rocks, stones and crystals and the animal realm as well as the Planet itself. When Saint Augustine said "Every visible thing in the world is put in the charge of an Angel," it was to Uriel and the myriad Angels that work with him that he referred.

We need the help of Uriel and the host of Angels and devas that work with him, more now than at any other time in the history of the world because we are in real danger of destroying the great creation that is the planet we live on. We need a miracle to reverse the damage that has already been done and prevent even more harm being done in the near future. Miracles come from the Angels and the Divine Power that works through them, and the great miracle that is so sorely needed now lies in the hands of Uriel.

So, the Earth needs Uriel, we need Uriel, but Uriel needs us, too: whenever we engage in work for the environment we are working with Uriel, and the value of that work is enhanced beyond measure if we consciously work with him. That may take the form of prayer or meditation, political action, conservation work and, especially, choices that we make about our lifestyle every hour of every day.

Of course, there are thousands of truly good and sincere people who are not aware of Angels, not consciously in tune with Uriel but still doing work of immense value to save species, raise environmental awareness or oppose the senseless destruction caused by greed. Their work is vital. Just imagine how much more powerful it might be if they asked for Uriel's help and blessing on their efforts. I am sure that Uriel does bless and help them, for they are doing his work whether they know it or not, but I suspect that they would find even greater strength if they worked in full awareness of this Archangel's power.

Some people will feel motivated to go out and pull up genetically modified crops or protest at the proposed destruction of a wood, others to sit at home and pray for the healing of the Earth. Both are doing Uriel's work. If we can integrate prayer and meditation with active campaigning where appropriate, it can be a potent combination. Whatever your personal approach to environmental issues, whether you are activist or a meditator or, indeed, both it is appropriate to invoke this Archangel and ask for his help.

Do not be discouraged by the thought that what you can do as an individual is too little to be of any use - all those little efforts from thousands of people add up to a great deal. The Dalai Lama once said "If you think you are too small to make a difference, try sharing a room with a mosquito!". Uriel reminds us that "If you are not part of the solution, you are part of the problem" and that to "walk lightly on the Earth" is a truly spiritual path.

I'm sure you will be able to think of many ways that you can minimize your personal impact on the Planet. However much or however little we can do in our personal lives to avoid waste, reduce pollution, resist harmful development, it is of value. Remember that every tea bag you put on the compost-heap, every piece of paper you recycle is like another feather added to Uriel's wings. If you engage in any Earth-healing work, whether it be dowsing, working with crystals, meditating or cultivating an organic garden, you are doing Uriel's work, too.

Else, for example, is a person who consciously meditates when she is tending her herb garden. One evening after she had been doing some planting in the herb garden earlier in the day, her thoughts turned to the newly-set plants and she immediately saw a great Angel bending quietly over them and enfolding them within his wings. When she went into the garden the following morning, the plants were bathed in a pool of golden light, quite different from any earthly light. Else says "The help we receive from the Angels on a daily basis is truly awesome, and a quiet 'thank you' is certainly called for." Uriel's other name, "Flame of God" tells us about another, tougher side to his nature, for he is usually identified as the Angel with a flaming sword who guarded the Eastern gate of the Garden of Eden after Adam and Eve were expelled from it and there is a powerful parallel here for us.

If we ruin the Earth - *our* Garden of Eden, will we ever be able to reclaim it?

But Uriel is a multi-tasking Archangel! As if looking after the very fabric of Planet Earth and all the living things on it were not enough responsibility for one Being, he is also the Angel of Resurrection and the Angel of Repentance. Here again he demonstrates the tough side of his nature, for he will accept only genuine repentance for past ill-deeds and will not accept mere lip-service. But when the wrongdoer is genuinely sorry and prepared to make amends Uriel shows utter compassion.

Perhaps we can see here some hope for the future of our ailing Planet.

If we truly repent of all the havoc we have wreaked on the Earth, we can count on Uriel to forgive us and help humanity to reverse the downward spiral of destruction and resurrect the beautiful Earth that once was our home.

A MEDITATION
WITH THE ARCHANGEL URIEL

As always, prepare for your meditation by making yourself comfortable and breathing quietly for a little while.

Now, imagine that you are sitting under a mighty tree. Feel its trunk supporting your back. Be aware of its great age and great strength. Imagine the roots going deep into the Earth and try to sense the energy that flows up and down between the roots, the trunk, the branches, to the ends of the tiniest twigs. Perhaps you can see some tiny creatures scuttling in the grass near your feet, or hear a bird in the branches above you. You feel the warm sun shining on your face and as you do so, recall that Uriel, the Regent of the Sun, is also the Guardian of the Earth, the trees, plants and all living things on it.

Gradually, you become aware that some unseen force is lifting you from the ground. You rise upwards, through the tree's branches. As you continue to rise up through the air you are aware of strong hands supporting you, and voice saying "I am Uriel. I am taking you to see the Earth from my perspective." You rise and rise, until you can see the Earth far below you. Uriel points out to you the grey clouds of smog, the dying forests, the dried-up lakes and river beds, the seas heavy with pollution and the Poles denuded of ice. He shows you the deserts encroaching on once-fertile land, the huge cattle-ranches where there was once rain-forest. As you watch, you become aware of Uriel's deep sorrow, and begin to share it.

Now Uriel shows you a vision of a perfect Earth: you look

down through the crystal-clear air and see the sparkling lakes and rivers, the seas teeming with life, you see great expanses of green forest, bordered by thriving little farms and smallholdings, you see busy villages and clean and lively cities. "Earth was once like this and can be again," Uriel whispers in your ear.

Gradually, you begin the long descent and after a while you find you are once more leaning against the tree-trunk. Be aware of the birds in the branches, of the myriad insects, of the plants growing in the shadow of the tree. Let your awareness reach out further to the other trees nearby, to other plants and any living creatures that are there. Perhaps there are butterflies, dragonflies, a timid vole, a scuttling beetle. Remember that Uriel is the Guardian of them all.

Finally, come back to your present surroundings. Perhaps, before you resume your day-to-day activities, you would like to take a few minutes to think about what you have just seen and what you can do to help Earth return to the beautiful vision that Uriel showed you.

SOME OTHER ARCHANGELS

Gabriel, Michael, Raphael and Uriel are the four most familiar and perhaps most important Archangels but they are by no means the only ones; there are many others celebrated in various traditions. There isn't room to consider all of them here - it would need another whole book! - but the following are some of those who seem to have the greatest relevance for us living in the twenty-first century.

AZRAEL

Azrael, or "He Whom God Helps" is known as the Angel of Death and his role overlaps that of Gabriel in accompanying the soul at the time of death and comforting those who grieve. Much early writing, both Jewish and Islamic, show Azrael as a terrifying figure, a sort of Grim Reaper, but in fact he is an Archangel of great compassion. Azrael and his host of Angel helpers are present in hospices and hospitals and wherever people are nearing their end. Eye-witness accounts from relatives, nurses and hospice volunteers often speak of a great Angel, or several Angels, hovering over a dying person's bed in the days and hours before their end and it seems clear that many of those about to die are aware of them and derive great comfort from their presence.

This moving story from Tessa illustrates this beautifully: Tessa's mother lived to be ninety-one but in the last decade of her life she became blind and developed dementia. Tessa found visits to the dementia unit heart-rending until one day she was prompted to look with her spiritual third eye and saw that the unit was full of Angels. They hovered on huge wings or stooped in loving comfort. All the patients had company, including those whose families never came to see them.

On her mother's last earthly day, Tessa sat with her asking for help. A great stillness filled the room and a solemn but gentle Angel was with them, tall and awe-inspiring. "Later," Tessa said, "I read of Archangel Azrael who accompanies the dying and comforts the grieving. Believe me, he exists!

I would never have thought that such a time could be so beautiful. Thank you, Azrael, and He who sent you."

CHAMUEL

Chamuel's name means "He Who Seeks God". He is one of the seven Archangels who stand in the Holy Presence, along with Gabriel, Raphael, Michael, Uriel, Jophiel and Zadkiel.

He is the Angel of Unconditional Love, who teaches us to love both others and ourselves, for we cannot truly love others until we do love ourselves. Chamuel can help us to overcome the negative feelings that prevent us from feeling good about ourselves.

Chamuel was present with Gabriel in the Garden of Gethsemane before the Crucifixion, and was one of the two Angels present at the Resurrection.

Through his great gift of love, he can comfort us through the darkest times and help us start life anew.

HANAEL

Hanael's name means "Glory of God" or "He who sees God" and he is another of the Archangels on the Tree of Life. He is one of the Angels who escorted the prophet Enoch when he was transported to heaven and transformed into the Archangel Metatron. He is the inspirer, the enthuser, the encourager who urges us to reflect the glory of the Divine by using all our talents and abilities to their fullest extent.

JOPHIEL

Jophiel, or "Beauty of God" is another of the seven Archangels of the Presence. He is sometimes identified as the Angel who drove Adam and Eve out of Eden, though most accounts agree that this was

Michael, while other texts describe him as a companion of Metatron. He teaches patience and helps us with mental and spiritual clarity so that we can overcome confusion and prejudice.

METATRON

Metatron is one of only two Archangels who have not existed since the very beginning of Creation but was once human. It is worth noting that his name does not end in the suffix -el, meaning "shining". Genesis tells us how the prophet Enoch was taken up by God and transformed into Metatron. Rabbinical lore considers him the highest and most powerful Archangel of all who sits on a throne alongside the Divine, so placing him even above the Archangel Michael. In the Kabbalistic tradition, he stands at the top of the Tree of Life. Unlike most of the other Archangels, the exception being Sandalphon, Metatron has a feminine companion called The Shekinah and together they represent wholeness or completion. Metatron and the Shekinah can inspire us to transcend our human limitations and remember that we are not human beings on a spiritual journey, but spiritual ones on a human journey.

RAGUEL

Raguel, or "Friend of God" is responsible for watching over the good behavior of Angels - a kind of heavenly Prefect! According to some traditions he is one of the Angels who took Enoch on a tour of the Cosmos before Enoch himself was transformed into the Archangel Metatron. He is also the Angel of true visions and helps us to see beyond illusion and realize the order underlying the universe.

RAZIEL

Raziel, or "Secret of God" is the "Angel of the Supreme Mysteries".

He is chief of the Thrones and appears surrounded by brilliant white fire, or simply as such a fire. In the Kabbalistic tradition he stands near the top of the Tree of Life, only one level lower than the great Archangel Metatron.

According to legend, he was the author of the "Sefer Raziel", a book in which all earthly and heavenly knowledge was set down. For us at the present time, he is the Archangel who helps us to understand spiritual truths and inspires the flashes of intuition that sometimes bless creative people.

REMIEL

Remiel is "The Lord of Souls awaiting Resurrection" and is though to lead souls to judgment. In some traditions he is also said to be one of the seven Archangels who stand before God, and is charged with spreading the instructions of the seven Archangels throughout Heaven and Earth.

SANDALFON

In the Kabbalistic tradition, the Archangel Sandalphon stands at the foot of the Tree of Life and is considered to be the twin brother of Metatron at the crown of the Tree. He is the only Archangel other than Metatron who has once been a human and we see once again that his name (Greek in origin) also ends in -on, rather than the -el that denotes the "Shining Ones". Like Enoch, the prophet Elijah was transported to Heaven and became the Archangel Sandalfon.

Also like Metatron, he has a feminine companion and helper, Auriel. Auriel is given by some sources as an alternative spelling of Uriel, though I think a truer interpretation is that she represents the feminine aspect of Uriel.

Sandalfon himself is to a large extent equivalent to the Archangel Uriel and some think that he is in fact the same Being under a different name. He exercises the same functions and inspires us in the same way to take care of our Planet. He is the Guardian of Earth and all living things, and he inspires the fairies, spirits and devas who inhabit and guard them.

The union of Sandalfon and Auriel working together for the protection of the Planet encourages us to undertake our ecological efforts in cooperation with others.

ZADKIEL

Zadkiel is another of the Archangels on the Tree of Life in the Kabbalistic tradition. His name means "Righteousness of God" and he is the Angel of benevolence and mercy. It was Zadkiel who stopped Abraham's hand when he was about to sacrifice Isaac. Zadkiel asks us to be merciful at all times, to ourselves as well as to others, and to refrain from acts of violence, even if only verbal aggression. We can call on Zadkiel when we feel angry and frustrated and ask him to transform our negative feelings into positive ones.

PART THREE

WORKING WITH ANGELS

WORKING WITH ANGELS

The Angels are ever-present, they ask nothing better than to work with us, help us and guide us in every aspect of our lives. But because we have free will, they need to be asked, to be invited into our lives. We need only ask for their presence and their help and we will receive it.

It helps, though, to make ourselves as open and receptive as possible. The more we make ourselves open channels for Angel energy, the more easily it can flow to us and through us, and the various exercises and techniques in this section of the book are all designed with this end in mind.

Some of the exercises are likely to appeal to you more than others: for example, if you see images easily in your mind's eye, you may find visualization easier than writing. Conversely, if words mean more to you than pictures, the journaling or dialoguing technique may turn out to be the way you can communicate easily with the Angels. I have set out here a number of different approaches, each of which has proved valuable for myself, my friends, and people attending the Angel workshops which I give from time to time, and I suggest that you try each of them until you find which one is most helpful in making contact with the Angels in your life. Maybe you will find all these approaches helpful at different times. I certainly do, depending on what I need to ask the Angels at a given moment.

But, more than any specific exercise or technique, it is our attitude towards the Angels, our way of approaching them that matters. If we are open and willing, if we are aware of their presence and influence, this is more valuable than any technique that has ever been devised.

An open mind and heart are all that is needed. All the same, in my experience it does help to make some conscious and deliberate effort to increase our own receptivity and sensitivity. The pressures of modern life do not make it as easy for us to be as open to Angelic influences as people were in - for example - the middle ages. So, maybe we need to try a little harder!

I think this is especially true when we first wish to work more closely with the Angels. We need to train ourselves, just as we might for any new activity, but the more we work with Angelic energies, the easier and more natural this becomes, until eventually it becomes second nature to us, like breathing out and breathing in.

ON SEEING ANGELS

"Seeing them isn't so much the crucial issue; it's being receptive to what they have to offer - being open and sensitive to their supporting, uplifting love."

EDGAR CAYCE

Many people have said to me that they wished they could see Angels. Some have said this quite simply, others expressed envy because I paint Angels and have, at times, had very clear visions of them. Some of these people clearly had a great deal of emotion invested in their desire for visible "proof" of the existence of Angelic Beings and, in some instances, have been trying really hard to see them.

To anyone who is doing likewise I would say "Stop trying!" Seeing an Angel is not a reward for effort, nor for goodness and the most unlikely people have seen them at the most unlikely times - just consider my own experiences as related in Chapter Two, for example. Angels mostly manifest when we least expect them, and I suspect that the harder you try to see them the less likely it is that you will. In fact, it is often true that the appearance of an Angel in somebody's life is a kind of "wake-up call" coming at a time when it is least expected and possibly not particularly welcomed.

But seeing is only one of the many ways in which we can become aware of their presence, and it is no more important or valid than any of the other ways. Just as we experience the world around us through all our senses, not through sight alone, so we can experience the non-worldly in a variety of ways, and different people are less or more likely to experience Angelic presences through sound, touch, smell or other means, depending on their dominant mode of perception. Our habitual ways of perceiving enter into play when we interact with non-physical Beings just as much as in our dealings with the physical world around us. Any of the physical senses may be a means of perceiving Angels, as well as thought, intuition, feeling and emotions.

Some people respond strongly to visual stimuli, others more to sound or touch. Some of us are very cerebral in our perception of the world, while some are much more influenced by their feelings. Psychologists have noted how our choice of words and our body language can pinpoint which mode of perception is our strongest and most habitual.

For example, in remembering something that happened a while ago, "visual" people may have a faraway look in their eyes as if they were seeing the event again (as indeed they are), while "hearing" people tend to tilt their head to one side as if re-hearing it. The cerebral person is more likely to say "I think" where the more intuitive person will say "I feel".

Some of us are more likely to say "I see" while others will say "I understand" and the "feeling" person may well touch you to emphasize a point. Try noticing these signposts when talking with friends, and work out which is their dominant mode of perception.

If you don't know which is your own habitual way of perceiving, you might want to try the following little test:

Think of a memorable occasion; it might be a time when you were very happy such as a wedding, a birthday, a first date, or a time when you were sad, or scared, or worried - it doesn't matter which so long as it was something that you remember very well. Now sit down somewhere quiet and think about that occasion. Have writing materials handy and, after a few minutes open your eyes and write down quickly what you remembered.

Was it something you heard - the wind in the trees, a certain piece of music, the words somebody said, the sound of laughter or crying?

Was it something you saw - people's faces, the color of the sky, a particular building? Something you touched - the texture of a dress, the feel of sand under your bare feet? Or do you remember how you felt emotionally that day? Or the smell of the perfume a friend was wearing?

Now write down:

What do you remember hearing?
What do you remember seeing?
What do you remember touching?
What do you remember tasting?
What do you remember smelling?
What do you remember feeling?
What do you remember thinking?

Which of those things sprang into your mind first?
Which did you find easiest to remember or most vivid?
Was there anything you DIDN'T remember?

The answers to those questions will almost certainly give you a clear idea of which is your strongest mode of perception, although you may find that you have two, equally strong ways of remembering . In that case you could ask an honest friend to take note of your speech and gestures for a while and see if one way emerges as strongest.

Psychologists have made in-depth studies of these differing modes of perception and apply them in many different ways, not least in education, where understanding which is a child's dominant mode of perception can make it far easier for teachers to help them absorb and remember facts. So, knowing that this can be so effective in earthly situations, how much more important it is to apply it to non-earthly ones!

Once you recognize your own dominant mode, it should be easier to be alert to Angels making their presence felt in the way that is most natural to you. After all, they want to make their presence felt so it makes sense that they will chose the most effective way!

Some people hear clear and direct messages. Yet others have been directed to write down information - sometimes the message has "arrived" in their minds and they have subsequently recorded it, sometimes they have found themselves writing - in longhand or at their keyboards - something which they were adamant did not originate with themselves. Some have experienced real physical sensations of touch or smell. Did you know that if you smell roses when there are no roses anywhere near an Angel has just passed by? Or it may be violets or jasmine. Many people believe, too, that finding a white feather is an indication that an Angel has passed by.

We need to exercise a little common sense regarding such forms of physical manifestation. If, for example, you smell sweet flowers when you know none are nearby, it makes sense to check that nobody has been using essential oils, perfumes or other scented products before you look for a metaphysical explanation. Similarly, if you have seagulls nesting on the roof or your neighbour has a dovecote, the appearance of white feathers is likely to have a more prosaic origin!

However, if a white feather appears where there is no logical

THE ARCHANGEL GABRIEL

THE ARCHANGEL MICHAEL

THE ANGEL OF JOY

THE ARCHANGEL ASRAEL

BLUE ANGEL

MICHAEL THE COMMANDER

THE ARCHANGEL URIEL

THE ANGEL OF ABUNDANCE

COSMIC ANGEL

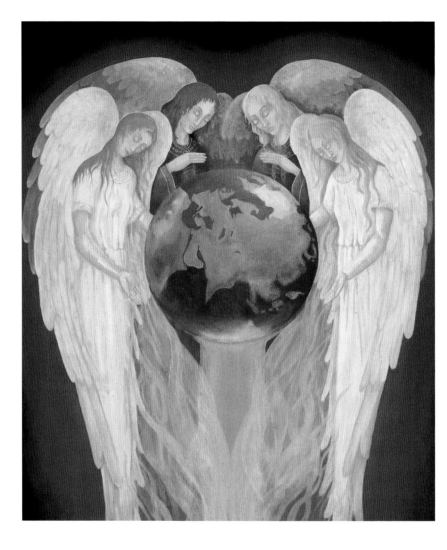

THE EARTH GUARDIANS

RAPHAEL THE HEALER

FOREST GUARDIAN

THE ANGEL OF LOVE

FIERY ANGEL

THE ANGEL OF THE DAWNING

OCEAN GUARDIAN

explanation, it can be taken as a legitimate sign that Angels are present. We also need, though, to be open to the fact that Angels do, at times, make use of mundane, earthly events if they need to attract our attention in this way.

Use your spiritual judgment - guided, perhaps by the wisdom of Archangel Michael - and you will know when this is so.

Clare's experience illustrates this beautifully: Clare was unsure whether to sell some shares in order to finance a course she wished to attend in order to become an Angel workshop teacher and asked the Angels if they would send her a clear sign that this was the right thing to do. During a walk in the countryside, she noticed a little white feather caught in some stinging nettles and carefully removed it, wondering if this was the sign and as she went on with her walk she found more and more white feathers and felt sure this was the sign she had asked for but later, when she got back to her flat some doubt crept in, partly because one of the feathers was gray. The following day she left her flat to go shopping, and when she came back she found a beautiful white feather carefully placed on a tread about half-way up her stairs. Clare says, "I was overcome with a sense of wild joy that I had been assured by these wondrous, loving Beings that I was making the right decision. That, YES, I had actually been contacted by Angels. Wow.

Phew. Hooray. THANK-YOU."

Clare paid attention to her doubts and used her wise judgment about them but when she found a feather where it could not have arrived accidentally she knew she could trust that as a genuine message.

And yet, there still persists a sense that to see an Angel is more valid, more "real" than any other kind of Angelic experience. I think that language often reinforces this prejudice: we talk of seers, of visions, visionaries and visualization but have few words to denote hearing, feeling, smelling or otherwise sensing the non-earthly. Consequently people who have had Angelic encounters that were not visual may find it harder to describe their experiences, or may feel that they were not as important as something they could see.

Then there are those who have flashes of knowledge that certainly came from no earthly source, or a powerful feeling of being protected in a dangerous situation. Angels may make themselves felt through our emotions, too, such as when we experience their great love and comfort at times of sadness or pain, or simply through a deep knowing.

I have met many people who have a very strong sense of Angels being present, although they have not seen, heard or physically felt anything.

Imagine sitting in a darkened room, or with your eyes closed: if somebody else enters the room, however quietly, you know they are there, as surely as if you could see them. Feeble though the comparison may be, this is how it can be with Angels - you don't see them but you are aware of them. You simply know they are there.

And perhaps simply knowing that the Angels are with us is the purest experience of all.

So, if you feel that your personal experience of Angels is incomplete or invalid because you do not see them as clearly as a figure on a television screen, please do not despair, but be aware of all the other ways that they can - and do - manifest. Be alert to all the possibilities but without striving. The very act of straining for an experience may be the one thing that prevents such an experience from happening.

A MEDITATION

Now that you know in which way you are most likely to know that Angels are present, let us go on a journey and put that knowledge to good use.

As always, make yourself comfortable and spend a few minutes quietly breathing.

Now, close your eyes and imagine that you are preparing for a very special meeting: you know beforehand that you are going to meet an Angel, perhaps more than one. You have no idea where this will take place or how it will unfold but you have two guides and helpers who you trust totally.

Gently, they tie a blindfold over your eyes and place mufflers over your ears. Taking you by the hands, they lead you forward and you sense that you are passing along a corridor and through a doorway.

You take a few more steps forward and your guides remind you to be especially aware of the manner in which you are most likely to perceive the Beings present in this place. As you attune your senses, they gently remove the blindfold and earmuffs and step back, leaving you to go forwards alone.

You are moved by the beauty you encounter, it may be by beautiful surroundings, it may be by heavenly music, it may be by sweet scents and gradually in the midst of this beauty you become aware of an Angelic presence.

Perhaps an Angel reveals itself to you in words, perhaps as a glowing light, perhaps as a beautiful figure or heavenly music. Perhaps you simply know that an Angel is there. Stay with this experience for as long as it feels right for you.

Now your guides come to lead you back to your earthly

surroundings and as they walk with you, you describe your experience to them.

As always, take a little time to return to the present and reflect on what you have just experienced.

You may wish to record your experience afterwards, in words, pictures or however feels most appropriate to you.

PRAYER AND MEDITATION

The most time-honored ways of communicating with Angels are prayer and meditation and there are many ways of approaching each of these practices.

Meditation tends to be associated with Eastern religions, but there is in fact a strong and long-established tradition of meditation among Christian mystics and many people practice meditation independently of any established religion.

There are many forms and techniques of meditation and it is worth exploring various practices until you find the one or ones that feel right for you. Do not be taken in by any teacher who claims that their way is the only right one! Many meditation techniques are aimed at stilling the mind, others at visualizing a spiritual Being or some spiritually inspiring scene.

The meditations that you will have found scattered throughout this book are mainly of the latter kind, while the brief section at the end of Chapter One is intended to help you prepare for whichever kind of meditation appeals most to you.

Meditations to still the mind are intended in the long run to quieten all our everyday worries and preoccupations so that, in the stillness, Spirit can speak to us. Exactly what that means will vary according to the spiritual tradition which the meditator follows. In the present context, remember that Angels are the messengers of the Divine and can fill our minds with God-inspired thoughts.

One of the simplest ways to still the mind is to focus on our breathing.

Again, there are many ways to do this, but the following is an effective one:

Once you are quiet and comfortable, pay attention to your in-breath. To help you do so, count each breath as you breath in, up to ten, then start again at one (this is just so that your mind does not get too tied up with remembering numbers!). Breath in, count "one" breath out; breath in, count "two", breath out; and so on. If you lose track, just start again at one.

After perhaps five minutes, switch to counting your out-breath: breath in, breath out, count "one", etc. It may be that, initially, this is all you will feel comfortable with, but if you want to continue, or at a later date, when you are familiar with this way of breathing, you may like to stop counting and simply pay attention to your breath: notice what it feels like as you breathe in, perhaps it feels cool on your upper lip? Notice your breath as it passes through your nose, notice how your lungs expand, how your diaphragm rises and falls. Notice what the breath feels like as you breathe out. Does it feel different from when you breathed in? Do this for as long as feels comfortable and right for you, starting perhaps with 10 minutes and sitting for 20 minutes or more as you become familiar with the practice.

I have described this kind of meditation at some length because it is valuable in its own right, as a way of clearing our minds of the stresses of daily life, the worries, the petty thoughts that plague us all the time.

Even if we had no spiritual aim in doing so it would be beneficial but in the present context the prime importance of clearing our minds in this way is so that we can hear what our Angels want to say to us.

Once the breathing meditation has allowed you to feel calm and tranquil, sit quietly and listen. In the silence, your Angels can speak.

Another traditional way to calm the mind is to continually repeat a sacred word, phrase or sound, known as a mantra. In some traditions this is done silently, within the mind and in others it is done aloud, perhaps as a chant. There are countless mantras but as a way of preparing us to hear the messages that our Angels wish to share, simply repeating the name of an Angel would be appropriate. If you know the name of your personal Guardian you might choose that, or perhaps the name of any Angel or Archangel that you would like to hear at a particular time. Once again, when you feel sufficiently calm and receptive, simply listen for whatever words or thoughts come into your head.

Meditations that aim at shown a mental image of an Angel or other spiritual Being are as many and varied as there are meditators and it would not be possible to describe all of them here, even if were possible for one person to be familiar with every variant. As I have already mentioned, you will find a number of them throughout this book, and there are many beautiful examples in other books, both those concerning Angels and those about meditation. Many spiritual teachers include such meditations in their workshops or gatherings and there is no reason why you should not invent your own. Simply sitting quietly and asking to be shown a particular Angel could be a way to begin.

Prayer is something to which many of us were introduced at an early age, perhaps as a simple grace before meals or a bedtime request for blessing and protection while we slept. When we reached school age we were probably introduced to more formal prayers though how little of such forms of prayer a young child can actually understand might be illustrated by some of the strange versions of the Lord's Prayer that little ones produce.

There are some very beautiful prayers that have been composed by saints and other devout people over the centuries. They may hold deep meaning for you, in which case it is excellent to use them just as they have been set down, or they may inspire you to use your own words in a similar way. At other times, it may be more meaningful to simply use whatever words come into your head and from your heart.

Is it right to pray to Angels? Or should we address our prayer directly to the Divine? Opinions differ, though I feel each is appropriate at different times. If, for example, you seek the help of a specific Angel or Archangel, it is surely right to ask that Angel directly, though at the same time remembering that even the most powerful Archangels are agents of the Divine.

Some people feel overawed by the prospect of addressing the Divine directly, and find it easier to so through the mediation of an Angel, or indeed a saint or the Virgin Mary. If this is true for you, then for you this is the right way to pray.

What words we use, how we go about it is not important. What matters is that we pray openly from the heart.

JOURNALING WITH ANGELS

Journaling, or dialoguing, with Angels is particularly helpful if you are a person who is happier working with words than with images, or if you are seeking quite specific help or advice.

The technique of "journaling" was developed in America in the 1970s as part of the human growth movement, and has been used as a way to contact the Higher Mind as a means of spiritual growth or the subconscious in psychotherapy, to "talk" to organs of the body in illness, and so forth, but it is also a wonderful way to get in touch with Angels and particularly to ask for guidance on specific issues.

It really could not be more simple.

Find a time and place when you will not be disturbed, and sit quietly with a pad of paper and a pen (or pens - I'll explain that later). If necessary, put a "Do not disturb" notice on your door and take the phone off the hook, or put on the answering machine if you have one. Take a few minutes to center yourself and still your mind by breathing quietly.

Now ask the Angels, and the Divine Spirit that works through them, to be with you. Do this aloud, or silently, whichever feels most appropriate and comfortable for you, and say that you are open and receptive to whatever messages they wish to convey to you. At first, this may feel very strange and artificial and you may not feel at all open and receptive, but persevere anyway. The more you do this the more natural it will feel.

Depending on what your purpose or need is, you might ask next to make contact with a specific Angel, or to be given guidance on a particular issue, or you might want simply to be open to whichever Angel chooses to communicate with you and whatever they have to say. Just state your wish clearly, either aloud or silently, as before.

Now take your pen and start writing. If you are seeking answers to a specific question or problem, write down the question, or if you are hoping to contact a particular Angel, write that Angel's name at the head of your page.

Whatever words then enter you head, write them down. Write as fast as you can without stopping to question what you are writing.

Don't worry about handwriting, spelling or punctuation, or even whether what you are writing seems to make sense at this point. You can always copy the text neatly later on, and the sense will almost always become apparent when you re-read it. If not, leave it for a few days and try again. Often an answer to your original question will jump off the page. You may find that there are times when nothing appears on the page, or enters your head. If so, try another time, in a calm and relaxed way without straining to "hear".

The pioneers of journaling suggest that you write with your non-dominant hand, i.e. the left if you are right handed or vice versa. This is because the two halves of the human brain function in different ways. The left hemisphere, or left brain is concerned with logic, intellect and verbal skills, while the right brain is the more intuitive, receptive side. The dominant hand is more closely linked to the logical left brain, so using the other hand helps to ensure that your conscious, logical, doubting mind does not get in the way. Writing with your non-dominant hand would be considered an ideal way of working by the originators of journal work, but we each need to find the system that suits us best. Many people find writing with the "wrong" hand so clumsy and slow that it impedes their ability to get the message onto paper as it is conveyed to them. I have tried both ways, and I ask people on my workshops to try both ways and explore which works best for them. So I would suggest that you do so too, and adopt whichever method allows you to write easily and quickly. What matters is not whether you are observing a given set of rules, but that you are writing in the way that makes it easiest for you to receive the messages you need at a particular moment.

Speed is another way of by-passing the logical mind, so write as fast as you can and trust that what you are recording is truly of

Angelic origin.

Even if it feels as if the words originate in your own mind, trust that the Angels are guiding your thoughts. Some people even seem to write without being conscious of a thought preceding or guiding what they write.

One of the most telling examples of this that I have ever seen took place at the first Angel workshop I ever led. One of the participants wrote fast and furiously for twenty minutes or so, and at the end of the session remarked that she had no idea what she'd written and could not read it without her glasses, which she did not have with her in the room, so she would be fascinated to find out later what she had recorded. I was touched by her implicit trust, which could serve as a wonderful lesson to all of us on how to go about this kind of work.

A slight variation on journaling is dialoguing. We go about this in just the same way, but using a question and answer format. You may have asked a question of the Angels, or a specific Angel, and found that you got quite a brief reply. If it feels appropriate, you may then wish to ask for clarification or put a subsidiary question, and so on. In this way a dialogue between you and the Angel will gradually emerge on the page. You might want to write "Q" and "A" to make it quite clear which is which when you read back what you have written later, or your own initial and an "A" for Angel, although I find that even without such distinctions I have no difficulty at all in distinguishing which is which: The Angels' style of writing is completely different to mine.

Another possibility is to use two different colored pens. However, I find that this, too, slows down the writing process. If you are happy and reasonably fast writing with your non-dominant hand, you could try a different colored pen in each hand: the dominant hand for your questions and the non-dominant one for the Angel's answers.

It helps to have a regular time to do this kind of work, just as it helps to have a regular time to meditate. Indeed, it could be very revealing to try journaling with the Angels immediately after a period of meditation.

Early in the morning is a good time for many people: the mind is fresh, not yet cluttered by the events and preoccupations of the day, but if you have children to be got ready for school, a journey to work or other responsibilities it may be a far from ideal time, and the other end of the day would be better for you.

Having established a regular time for your writing, be aware that there may also be times when you need to be spontaneous and grab a pen and paper to record an Angel message when you are least expecting it! When I began to work in this way, I sat at the same time each day, and I was quite clear before I began about the issue I wanted to examine, and/or the Angel from whom I wished to request guidance. After a while, though, I found that an inner voice would sometimes insist that I put down whatever I was doing and pick up a pen! Or that I would "hear" snatches of Angel messages or dialogues, and need to take a pen and focus on them in order to distinguish them more clearly.

Another possibility is that more than one Angel may wish to speak with you, or they may wish to speak with each other on your page. You may end up having a three (or more) sided conversation. This seems to happen when you need help or guidance around complex issues that can best be solved with help from two or more Angels.

Sometimes people like to do this work with a partner: one asks the question(s) or names the Angel from whom they would like to receive guidance, and the other person writes. Then they reverse roles. This can be valuable if you are afraid that your feelings about a particular issue are so strong that they are clouding your ability to be a clear channel.

Obviously, this requires total trust on the part of both people, and can only be undertaken where both people are committed to the Angelic path.

I have been asked quite often whether it is possible to do this work on a computer or word-processor. If you can type faster than you can use a pen, this might be the way for you but somehow the contact of pen with paper seems to be more intimate and personal. Finally, remember that Angels are messengers of the Divine, and that when you receive a message from them it is truly Divine guidance.

ANGEL CARDS AND ORACLES

Angel cards can be a great help in "tuning in" to Angel energy, or asking for guidance on specific issues. They may be particularly appropriate if the journaling technique does not appeal to you. For example, I know that some people find it difficult to believe that something they have written down themselves did not emanate from their own mind - even though it may be from some higher level of mind. To ask for guidance and receive an answer that they have not written themselves can be reassuring. Many people, though, find it helpful to use both of these methods at different times.

There are any number of different packs of cards available, ranging from small, simply illustrated cards to quite elaborate sets, some accompanied by books, and each intended to be used in a slightly different way.

The simplest Angel Cards are the tiny ones that originated from the Findhorn Foundation several decades ago. These each have on them the name of an Angel and a simple, often humorous, drawing illustrating some aspect of that Angel's energy. They are used very simply, by selecting a card at random to discover which Angel, what kind of energy, is to guide you at that particular moment. Many people choose a card every morning to see which Angel is to guide them through that day. Another way to use them is to select a card at the beginning of a new enterprise, or the start of a healing session, workshop, meditation, or any other time when Angelic guidance is needed. The choice of cards may seem to be random, but when you work with Angels and trust their guidance you discover that there is no such thing as chance. Time after time, the card selected will be totally appropriate to the person who has picked it at that precise moment in time.

Here, as in so many other ways, the Angels often show their sense of humor!

You may, for example, find that you have drawn the Angel of Patience, just when you were feeling particularly impatient, or the Angel of Responsibility when you'd really like to let go of all your responsibilities. The point, of course, is that the cards remind you that this Angel is there to help you through the difficulty.

Some sets of cards are more complicated, carrying an affirmation or guidance connected with the Angel each card represents. They may come with a book containing longer texts than could be printed on a card, and often with suggestions about different ways you might use the cards.

For example, you may simply choose a card each morning in the same way as with the Findhorn set, or a single card to ask for guidance on a specific question. Many of these packs, though, contain suggestions for more complex combinations of cards that enable the questioner to ask for guidance on matters that cannot, perhaps, be answered quite so simply.

You may want to try out, or at least look at, several packs before you decide which you would find most helpful, but unfortunately, many of the boxed sets of cards-plus-book are sold shrink-wrapped so unless your bookshop has a sample set you can examine, I would suggest asking friends who already have a set if you might try them out before you buy your own.

That way you might avoid making expensive mistakes as I have done in the past! Whichever set you may eventually choose, it should resonate with your personality, tastes and needs. Do the pictures appeal to you? Does the way in which the guidance is expressed feel appropriate to you? If there is a book with the set, is it easy to refer from the cards to the book? Take time to consider all these things, because if any of these elements do not feel right for you, you are unlikely to make the best use of the set.

Whichever set of cards you may choose to work with, it is a good idea to spend a little time in preparation before turning to them. Find a quiet place, and a time when you will not be interrupted, sit still and focus on your breath for a few minutes to still the mind. Then focus on the question you wish to ask, or the issue about which you are seeking guidance. The more clarity you can bring to formulating your question, the greater the possibility that you will receive clear guidance in response. Ask the Angels to be present and to guide your choice of cards, then allow your mind to be open and receptive to whatever guidance you may receive. Shuffle the pack thoroughly - many people feel that this imparts something on your own energy to the cards - before choosing your card or cards. Some people like to choose a card with their eyes shut, others find that looking at the pack fanned out helps them to make a choice. Do whichever feels most appropriate for you.

Sometimes the guidance received via the cards may not seem clear. You may feel it is not relevant to the question you asked, or too vague, etc. If this happens, you may want to ask a subsidiary question for clarification but please beware of falling into the trap of feeling a little petulant, a little hard-done-by and thinking "I don't like that one, I'll choose another". It's so easy to do but it negates the principle of asking for guidance. Besides, the next card you pick may be even less welcome! Often the best course is to make a note of the card, or cards, you have picked and return to them a day or so later, at which point the message will often be transparently clear.

Angel cards - whichever ones you prefer - can also be used by more than one person if they are seeking guidance on issues they have in common. For example, if several people are embarking jointly on some new venture, when a group meet to pray or meditate together, or if partners need guidance about some aspect of their relationship.

If you are working with other people, it is even more important to be absolutely clear about what you intend to ask. Determine this between you before you approach the cards, as well as how you are going to handle the cards and make your choices. For example, will one person shuffle and another pick a card, or will each person shuffle in turn? If you are going to use more than one card, will each person take it in turn to select one?

Will you read the guidance out loud, or will you pass the cards or book to each person to be read silently? Sort all these things out in advance so that there is no need for discussion or interruption once you begin to work with the cards themselves. Take time to tune in to each other, as well as to the Angelic energies, and ask the Angels to guide you collectively to a clear understanding.

Allow time for discussion after the reading: people may interpret the cards in slightly different ways, or it may well be that some aspects of the guidance received will be more appropriate to one person than another.

Talking through what has emerged from the cards can be valuable, as each person contributes their own understanding: what is unclear to you may be perfectly lucid to somebody else, and vice versa.

The idea of using cards to seek Angelic guidance may appear a bit simplistic, even frivolous, and of course it could be so if we approach it in a frivolous frame of mind. When working with cards, it is very important to do so with the right intent, not as a game or a form of "fortune telling". If you trust that this is simply one of the many ways in which the Angelic realms can communicate with you, and use the cards with an open mind and a pure heart they will, indeed, act as a bridge between you and the Angels.

CHANNELING WITH THE ANGELS

I referred briefly to channeling in the chapter on journal work, but it is worth exploring this a little more, even though fewer people will feel drawn to this than to guided writing.

Voice channeling requires the practitioner to put aside their own personality and thoughts and allow their vocal cords to be used by another Being. Some bring through messages while speaking in their normal voices while others speak in voices totally different from their own. Some channels have no consciousness or memory after a session of what has been said through them, some can remember clearly, others vaguely. It also, obviously, calls for one or more other people to be present to hear what is being said and, in some instances, record it on tape or in writing.

This calls for great integrity on the part of the channel and a measure of discernment on the part of the listener. Most of what I am going to say next is addressed to you as a possible listener, even if you think you would never be likely to act as a channel, though most channels I know did not deliberately set out to do this work. They were astonished, and sometimes frightened, to find it happening.

Should you find such a thing happening to you, do not take fright, but do take steps to be quite certain that you know who is really speaking through you. Remember also that you have free will: if it distresses you to act as the voice for another intelligence *you do not have to do so.* If you *are* willing to act as a channel you also have the right to be in control of the situation in which will you will, or will not, do so. You do not have to give voice on behalf of another Being when you feel it is inappropriate, such as in a social setting, or when there is a chance that somebody present will be frightened or disturbed by the event, or even when it is simply not convenient, such as when you are cooking or driving on the motorway!

However, I suspect that no Angel or other Being that is coming from the Highest Light would attempt to speak through any channel at a time when it would not be right to do so.

If you are listening to a channel you should also be certain who is really speaking through them. Unfortunately, if it is possible for discarnate Beings of great wisdom to speak through human mouthpieces, it is also possible for other intelligences whose intention is far from benevolent, to do so. If you have any doubt whatsoever about the origin of a voice that is being channeled, challenge the speaker. Ask who is speaking and whether they come from the Highest Light. Ask this three times. You should get a positive, unequivocal answer each time.

Without wishing to be judgmental, I feel bound to say that some channels do seem to be misguided and are not bringing through messages from any other intelligence but are speaking from some part of their own mind. Now, if that part of their mind is pure and working for the Angels, and if the messages are enlightening and helpful to those who hear them, then there is little or no harm in this except, possibly, of inflating the importance of the message. After all, if it came from Dwahl Khul it must be more important than if it came from Joe Bloggs, mustn't it? (There is also some risk of inflating the ego of Joe Bloggs! In my experience the true channels who are bringing through information of great purity and importance are self-effacing and genuinely humble.)

By no means all the people who are genuinely channeling at the present time are channeling Angels: many claim to be channeling Ascended Masters or wise souls who have previously lived on Earth. There are, though, some who are voicing Angels and Archangels and bringing through deeply moving and relevant guidance in this way. But as more and more people open their minds and hearts to the Angels and declare their willingness to work with them for the good of humanity and of the Planet Earth, I think we will find more people who do act as mouthpieces for Angels and Archangels. They could be said to be working with the Archangel Gabriel in a very direct way.

ANGELS AND CREATIVITY

The Angels delight in our creativity. Few things please them more than to see us using the gifts given to us by the Creator.

You don't have to be "an artist" to be creative! If you sew a dress or knit a beautiful sweater, if you tend a garden or make your surroundings harmonious you are being creative. If you bake a delicious cake, you are expressing your creativity, so do not be afraid to ask the Kitchen Angels (yes, there really are Kitchen Angels!) to be by your side.

When you handle plants, tune in to the Angels of the plant kingdom, who are often called Plant Devas. Every plant, indeed every blade of grass, has its own Angel and when we are aware of their presence and work in harmony with them, the plants in our care will flourish. When we walk in a garden that has been created in conscious co-operation with the Angels, we feel that harmony. So it is with the homes of people who are in touch with Angels: there is an extra dimension of peace.

To turn to more formal expressions of creativity: many artists throughout the ages have worked consciously with the Angels in many media - music, poetry, dance, painting, sculpture, etc. Over and over again one hears of tunes that come fully-formed into the composer's head, poems that were dictated to the poet, and so on. A friend who writes children's stories with a spiritual content says "I hear them being read aloud - I just feel like the scribe." Surprising and beautiful things can happen when we work freely in whatever medium we feel drawn to, without focusing too much on the end result. I love the following story that came to me from Mira, who is a yoga teacher. Mira had a car accident which resulted in severe whiplash that prevented her from teaching yoga for six months and during that time she became very depressed, in fact she described that period as her "dark night of the soul." Her friends and family supported through this bad time, and sometimes at night she was aware of a small bright light in her bedroom, with no obvious source. During recovery when the depression was beginning to lift, she got her watercolor paints out to "play" with. One day she painted, as she thought, a sunrise but when she turned the painting upside down she discovered to her delight that she had painted an Angel. Since then she has painted in a very free manner, without any intention to produce a result, and when the painting is finished, images become obvious which she had not consciously created.

Notice the words "play" and "without any intention to produce a result". The very openness that they imply is what allows the Angels in.

Sometimes the Angels involve themselves in the actual, physical making of a work: in the church of Santissima Annunzione in Florence there is a very early fresco of the Annunciation painted by a monk who had no previous experience of art - he is said to have completed it in one night with the assistance of an Angel. Now, I've learnt to paint frescoes and actually painted a dancing Angel on the wall of an Italian church, so I know from experience that without such help this Annunciation panel would represent several months' work by a team of skilled artisans! We might dismiss this as a pious legend were it not for the fact that, very soon, miracles began to be associated with this painting. Other churches commissioned painters to make copies, and there are many very similar frescoes in other Italian churches... but no miracles have ever been attributed to them. Many of them are more beautiful, more skillfully executed, but they do not hold the Angelic energy.

It is not only in the past that miracles have been associated with paintings of Angels: for example, the paintings of American Angel artist Andy Lakey have frequently been found to be healing and he is but one among many.

I always ask for Angelic help and guidance when I sit down to paint (as I do when I sit down to write) and I have, on a few rare and precious occasions, had the experience of my paintbrush moving without my volition.

The images that come in this way are always powerful and charged with energy, and they emerge on the canvas with great ease and speed, even though my usual method of working is rather painstaking and slow. More often, though, help comes in the form of images forming very clearly in my mind.

A potter takes a lump of clay, the very stuff that our Planet is made of, and fashions it into an object of beauty or usefulness, often both together. The woodworker and turner do likewise. A sculptor takes stone from the mountains or metals from deep inside the earth and transforms it into a lasting work of art. How blessed they are that the planet furnishes them with such beautiful materials, and how blessed are we that we can enjoy the fruits of their skill. Surely Uriel and his host of Angels delight to see it too.

Singing is perhaps the form of creativity that brings us closest to the Angels and the closeness is all the more precious because, as with dance, we need no instrument, no equipment in order to sing. Our instrument is our own body and breath. When we sing, we are doing Angels' work. We are sharing the eternal song of the Seraphim. This is true whenever we sing, whether it is alone or with others, though singing in a choir, hearing the harmony that many voices can create, being part of that, is perhaps the nearest we can get to what choirs of Angels experience. We cannot know, but we can trust, and we can ask the Angels to bless our endeavors.

It is but a short step from singing to playing an instrument, another way of creating wonderful harmonies. There are countless paintings of Angels playing instruments, often accompanying a choir of singing Angels and we may imagine their pleasure when we do likewise. There is a chapel in Siena which has 16 Angel-musicians painted on the ceiling, accompanying 16 dancing Angels and I like to imagine an Angelic orchestra playing for the dancers throughout eternity. Certain instruments are particularly associated with Angelic music-making, trumpets, all kinds of stringed instruments and the harp perhaps most of all but it doesn't matter what kind of instrument you play so long as you create beautiful harmonies to uplift the soul, or comfort those who are distressed. There is a growing body of evidence that demonstrates how much music can help those who are ill, even shortening recovery times, reducing the need for analgesics, etc. If you should feel called to do this kind of work it would truly be co-operating with the Angels of Healing.

Dance is a form of creativity that needs no instrument but the human body. The ability and the instinct to dance is with us from birth: watch a small child dancing and you will see the purest expression of joy. Of course, some people undertake long and arduous training in order to dance in specialized ways, and I for one give thanks for the pleasure they bring to those who watch them, but everybody can dance if they allow themselves to retain the holy innocence of a child.

Dance was once acknowledged as an act of worship, from the ecstatic dances of the followers of Dionysus to the temple dancers of Egypt and from David dancing in front of the Ark to dances performed in Christian churches in mediaeval times. And remember that when we dance, we are nearer to flying than at any other time in our earthly lives. The following poem, written by my friend Grace after she had attended a weekend dance workshop, expresses this perfectly:

"Soaring, flying, sailing on Bach,
Ecstatic, uplifting.
Uplifted,
My heart dances as much as my feet.
This music feels like home,
This dance is where I belong,
Free as a cloud,
Soaring like a lark,
Shining like a star,
Flying like an Angel.
Dancing with Angels - yes,
Only Bach is right for that."

In this instance one form of creativity, dance, gave rise to another, poetry.

I am sure there are many other ways of expressing the creative impulse that I have forgotten and if one of them is your chosen medium, I ask your forgiveness, but any and every form of creativity is more rewarding if it is undertaken in conscious co-operation with our Angels.

So if you engage in any form of creativity whatsoever - and I hope that you do, for your life is likely to be the richer for it - always ask the Angels to be with you before you begin.

That way, you will be a co-creator with God.

WHEN BAD THINGS HAPPEN

A question that is often asked is "Why does God allow bad things to happen?" Where were the Angels on September 11th 2001? Where were the Angels when the tsunami struck South East Asia? Where were they when a much-wanted baby was born with a severe handicap or a beloved wife and mother died young?

The answer, I believe, is that Angels are concerned with our spiritual well-being rather than our physical survival.

Certainly, there are well-authenticated accounts of Angelic involvement where people have survived terminal illness or escaped from apparently fatal accidents. I believe that in such cases there are always spiritual reasons why that person did not die: perhaps they had important work to do, perhaps they had lessons still to learn on Earth, perhaps there were lessons that they could teach to others. Indeed, their very survival could be seen as a lesson.

One thing we should always remember is that death is not a tragedy for the person who has died: it is a transition to a different state and there will be Angels there to guide them, chief among them being the Archangels Gabriel and Azrael. The tragedy is felt by those who remain here, but if they are aware of the Angels surrounding them with love, if they can comprehend a little of the transcendental state to which the dead person has been translated, it can ease their pain. Comforting the bereaved is a special function of the Archangel Azrael and the personal Guardians of everybody involved will have a major part to play, too.

The following story is a powerful illustration of how an Angel can bring comfort in the face of tragedy:

Jenny's family were all in shock following a terrible car crash in which three young men, including her younger daughter's boyfriend, had been killed and her older daughter's boyfriend injured. Three days after the crash Jenny had an overwhelming experience of seeing an Angel. She was woken from her sleep by an incredibly bright light. Coming out of the light was a young man wearing what she described as a short toga, although she could only see him as a silhouette because the light was so blinding. He appeared to be 22, the same age as the three dead boys and was carrying a branch which had been cut from a tree but was still flourishing.

Jenny was filled with fear and could hear her heart beating, but when she sat up the vision disappeared. For the next two nights she felt a strong presence in her bedroom, but was so frightened she denied it and after two nights it was no longer there. She felt very unsettled and three days after she saw the Angel, she went for a walk in the woods to try to calm herself and analyze what had happened. In the woods she heard a voice telling her not to analyze, but to relax and open her mind, and she heard the words "You can cut off the branch but it still flourishes. Death is not the end." The voice told her to go and comfort one boy's parents with this message, but it took her another three days before she could find the courage to do so, because they were a very reserved couple and she did not know how they might react. They did, though, accept the words of comfort and she told them that death was not the end, and they would see David again.

Talking about it several years later, Jenny likened both the blinding light and her great fear to many biblical accounts of people's reactions when confronted by an Angel, and the fact that such encounters so often changed people's lives. Before this encounter, Jenny had no interest in Angels and it took several more years before she even realized that the Being she had seen was, in fact, an Angel, though she immediately recognized that it was a messenger. Once she connected with the Angels she made major changes in her life, which led to her becoming a yoga teacher and Reiki healer after an earlier career as the owner of a beauty salon. .

In the aftermath of the tragic car crash, this Angel not only brought comfort to several families, but profoundly changed at least one person's life.

Azrael, like all Archangels, may work through the host of Angels under his command and also through human intervention. The same is true of Raphael. The doctors, nurses, rescue workers, firefighters and all who speed to the scene of a major disaster are doing Angels' work, whether they know it or not.

The overwhelming response of people from all over the world to the Asian tsunami in 2005 is another example of how the Angels inspire us and open our hearts. Never in human history has so much money been given by so many people in such a short time and that, of course, was in addition to all the volunteer helpers who rushed to the scene, and continued with relief and rebuilding long after the event.

On the afternoon of 11th September 2001, I received a very brief and urgent message from a friend with contacts in America: "Something terrible has happened in New York. I don't have the details but a lot of people have been killed. Please will you meditate and pray." I sat down to meditate at once and as soon as I closed my eyes I saw the entire sky full of Angels, thousands of Angels, wave upon wave of them flying Westwards, i.e., in the direction of the U.S.A. from Devon, where I live. They were all blue, which is the colours I most often see Angels in response to crises. When terrorist bombs hit London in July 2005, I saw almost exactly the same sight in meditation, though the Angels were fewer in number.

So what do the Angels ask us, as human beings, to do in times of crisis?

First of all, to pray. It need only take a second to ask for Angelic help.

Next, if there is anything practical that we can do to alleviate suffering, to do it. Then pray some more. In the aftermath of any catastrophe, whether it affects one person or thousands, relay the Angels' messages of comfort to everybody who is affected, though in doing so we must not appear to be pushing our beliefs on to other people: be sensitive to people's feelings and wait for the right moment. Just listen, and your Guardian will tell you when to speak and when to keep quiet.

If something terrible has happened through the action of one person or a group of people, as in the case of murder, assault, rape or terrorist attacks, remember to pray for the perpetrators as well as the victims. Ask your Angels to help you to love instead of hate.

Then you will be truly doing Angelic work.

WORKING WITH ARCHANGEL GABRIEL

It is, perhaps, not quite as easy to define how we might work with the Archangel Gabriel as it is with some of the other Archangels. For example, the work that Uriel asks us to do is practical, earthly, related to our daily lives. But if we consider the various roles that Gabriel fulfils, and look at each of them separately, it becomes clearer how we can co-operate with him in various ways.

First, Gabriel is known best as the Divine Messenger, so how can we become part of that? I think, primarily by being fully alert and open to receive whatever messages Gabriel wishes to convey to us. These may not necessarily be obvious: we are not all granted the privilege of directly hearing or seeing a great Archangel, but there are many other ways in which we can receive Gabriel's "wake-up call". It may be through an apparently chance meeting, a book that we feel compelled to read, a poem, a painting, a piece of music, a series of events that might be called coincidences. Any of these may tell us something the Angels want us to hear. Pay attention, too, to your dreams; the Angels often use them as a means of sending us messages.

Then, having heard the message, we need to act upon it! If there is anything in our lives that needs to change, we need to ask Gabriel to give us the courage to make that change.

We may sometimes be asked to take on the role of messenger ourselves. It may be that something we say opens a door for somebody else or that sharing our own experience of Angels gives another person the courage to talk about how Angels have manifested in their life. The first time I ever led an Angel workshop, I scheduled a "sharing time" when people could talk about their own experiences, and one person after another said that it was the first time they had felt able to share their story without fear of ridicule, misunderstanding or even hostility.

Secondly, we know that Gabriel is closely associated with pregnancy and birth, so midwives, obstetricians, health visitors and everybody who supports pregnant women are doing Gabriel's work. If you are one of them, consider how much more powerful your work will be, how the mothers and babies in your care will be blessed, if you are consciously co-operating with the Archangel Gabriel. If you have time before attending a pregnant woman, try to meditate upon Gabriel beforehand. If not, at least offer a quick prayer. If you are not a professional, but perhaps the friend or relative of a woman about to give birth you can support her in just the same way. If she is receptive to the idea, you can discuss this with her and maybe even take a small picture or medallion of Gabriel into the birthing room. If she is not likely to receive your ideas kindly simply meditate, pray and keep quiet!

Thirdly, remember Gabriel's role at the other extreme of life, as the phychopompus or Guide of Souls. Working with Gabriel is a blessed thing to do if you care for terminally ill patients, volunteer in a hospice or sit with a friend or relative who is approaching the end of their earthly life.

Simply going about your work in the knowledge of Gabriel's presence will help to bring calm to the dying soul. People in their final days and hours are often aware of the presence of Angels, even if they have given little or no thought to them before and are likely to be receptive to anything concerning Gabriel that you feel it is right to share with them. Even when somebody has apparently lapsed into unconsciousness they may be aware of what you are telling them.

Remember, too, that Gabriel is there to comfort the bereaved. If you work with the dying, you will often be called upon to comfort and counsel relatives and friends, so call on Gabriel to help you say the right thing - which might be nothing at all! A warm hug, a listening ear might be the most appropriate response, but if you ask for Gabriel's guidance you will know what to do.

WORKING WITH ARCHANGEL MICHAEL

Working with the Archangel Michael can seem like a tough assignment. For example, we can never aspire to become Commanders of the Heavenly Host! The most we can do in relation to that particular role of this mighty Archangel is to be willing to do the Angels' bidding. Remember that all Angels ultimately take their orders from Michael, so that anything which any Angel may require of us humans is the very end of the chain of command that originates with Michael.

In relation to Michael's other functions though, there is much we can do.

Bearing in mind that Michael cuts through ignorance, that he is the implacable enemy of greed, that he is the wisest of wise judges, we can follow his example in our own small ways.

We can make it our business to seek out spiritual truths: read the books, go to the talks, take part in the workshops - and then, which is the harder part, apply what we have learnt to our daily lives. Sometimes this will involve making difficult decisions, but we do not have to do this alone; we can call upon Michael as well as our personal Guardians to guide us. The meditation at the end of the chapter on the Archangel Michael might be helpful at such times.

Michael asks us to be discriminating about the people we choose to associate with. This does *not* mean being judgmental, as in "I'm right, he's wrong," or "I'm good, she's bad." Rather, it may mean asking ourselves whether the company of a particular person, the conversations we have with them, the activities we share, are compatible with the moral and spiritual choices that we have made, or whether they are holding us back in some area of our spiritual growth. To sever old friendships can be one of the most difficult and painful things we are called on to do upon our journey, but we can ask Archangel Michael to both help us make such decisions and to ease the hurt of doing so.

Michael's wise judgment is especially valuable in situations where there is conflict. Few of us are called on to make major decisions in situations such as international tension or warfare, but we can pray that national leaders will be guided to make wise decisions, and if they do not, we can pray that we will be given the gift of compassion, so that we do not judge them harshly.

It is rare for an Archangel as exalted as Michael to intervene where there is conflict between two individuals: more often, their personal Guardians will act upon his orders, but the following story, which I will let Rowanna tell in her own words, shows that he may occasionally step in defuse a dangerous situation.

"I was verbally abused in the street by an angry neighbor, so viciously that I was still feeling shaken and distressed the following day. More than that, I had a strong feeling that the woman was attacking me psychically. I sat to meditate on the situation and tried first of all to send love and understanding to the angry woman, but felt she was unreachable. I thought 'I need to put something between her and me,' and immediately, before I had time to think what that might be, I saw the Archangel Michael as he appears in Ishvara's painting, robed in red and purple. I then became aware that the picture had become double-sided, facing both towards myself and my adversary. It then became four pictures, one on each side of me. Then the colours in the painting began to blend like a vertical rainbow. The blue closed over my head, the golden yellow beneath my feet and I had a feeling of warmth and security which was still there several hours later. Subsequently, I felt that I was completely protected from psychic attack or anything else that the angry woman could do."

In more intimate areas of conflict, we may be in a position to take the role of mediator. It may be in a dispute between husband and wife, employer and employee, parent and child, it may be a situation where tension has arisen between different groups in our local community. If, with Michael's help, you can take the heat out of the situation, remain impartial but sympathetic to the feelings of both sides, you will truly be doing the work of Angels.

WORKING WITH ARCHANGEL RAPHAEL

In everybody's life there will come a time when healing is needed, for oneself or for a loved one. This might be because of physical illness, injury, emotional or mental distress or relationship problems and in any of these situations Raphael is ready to help us. We can ask for healing for strangers, too, as well as for groups, countries, towns, etc. For example, when there are troubles in society, a disturbed situation in our home town, and for world problems such as wars or famine though in these latter instances there are other Archangels who we should involve as well.

It is very appropriate to call on Raphael for help when you are ill, or when somebody you know is ill. If you are ill or hurt yourself and are about to receive treatment, it would be ideal to make time for a prayer or meditation before each treatment, or before an operation or hospital visit, as well as asking for healing on a daily basis. Do this in the absolute faith that your request will be heard and acted upon.

When I fractured my arm very badly some years ago I went to a rather special lady called Liz Dolton for healing, as the bone was not knitting together and I was being threatened by the consultant with the prospect of a bone-graft. At the first of these sessions I was physically aware of other Beings in the room: I could feel dozens of hands gently touching me all over and Liz, for all her great gifts, has but one pair of human hands! At the end of that sessions she confirmed that there had indeed been a whole crowd of Angel helpers present, also that they had commented to each other "Oh, the poor thing, she's broken her wing!" My arm healed strongly and I did not need a bone-graft.

We can ask for help with absent healing too. This can be a great comfort when we are far from somebody we would like to help. There are absolutely no "rules" to go by: I simply sit quietly, hold a mental picture of the person who is in need of help and ask for Raphael or the most appropriate angel to bring healing to them. I know other people who like to put a photo on their altar, or write the person's name on a piece of paper and place it under a crystal You can do this for a friend, relative or other loved one, or for a stranger if you have been asked for help. Many churches and healing groups keep a list of names for whom healing prayers are asked, and I know people who simply circulate such requests among their friends so we may be seeking help for people we don't know. In this age of electronic communication this can be done so quickly and effectively. As well as praying or meditating for another person, you might find out when they are due for any treatment and focus healing attention on them at the appropriate time.

For example, when my sister was due for a major operation, a whole circle of friends meditated at the time she was due to be in the operating theatre. When we talked to each other afterwards, we found that most of us had had a nearly identical experience of seeing two great blue angels standing behind the surgeon with their wings folded round him. (This is an image which I have since found occurs frequently in similar situations.) The operation was successful. Had it not been, my sister might not be with us today.

If you are a doctor, nurse, physiotherapist, alternative therapist, healer or involved in any way with the care of those in need of healing ask the angels, and the Archangel Raphael in particular, to bless your work each day before you start. Equally if you are a counsellor, therapist, mediator, etc., working with people whose relationship is in trouble, call on Raphael at the start of each day's work. Then tune in to the Angels at the start of each session. Try also to tune in to the patient's or client's guardian Angel, too, and ask for their presence. And don't forget to thank the Angels and Archangels afterwards!

A lovely example of a therapist working with the angels is Sarah, an osteopath who is regularly helped by an angel in her healing work. Her angel helper first manifested in the form of flashing lights around her right eye, which alarmed her sufficiently to have her eyes examined by an ophthalmologist, a wise decision, as flashing lights can be a symptom of detached retina. Having found that there was nothing at all wrong with her eyes, Sarah sought the real reason and, by means of automatic writing discovered that they signalled the presence of her Angel helper, who is called Angelica.

Angelica helps Sarah during treatment sessions, mainly by means of lights, usually blue or purple or a voice in her head directing her to the part of the body she should work on next, which is not always where she would expect in the light of the patient's apparent problems. Often she needs to do nothing more than place her hands on the area and the results are such that the patient needs no further treatment, even when their problem would normally need a number of sessions to correct it. Sarah says "It often feels that I just need to stand aside when treating and become a channel." Angelica also gives Sarah information about new patients before they arrive. Sarah writes a question about the patient, and by way of answer Angelica dictates information about their health, etc. The information given is not always related to the osteopathic treatment they have booked and is sometimes quite surprising. For example, Sarah was told that a woman patient was pregnant, although the woman had been diagnosed as having an early menopause. Sarah did not see this lady again for six months, when she learnt that she was indeed expecting a daughter. Sometimes Angelica also describes the person, and Sarah recognises them as soon as she sees them in the waiting room.

Before I met Sarah for the first time, she asked Angelica if the angels had a message for me and was told "Yes, Sarah, tell Ishvara that we love and support her in what she is doing. Love to her." She was also given information about two minor health problems which I was able to tell her was totally accurate, and after asking if the angels had any words of support for me, was told: "Love and Light, Peace and Grace. She requires no other support as she is already receiving all that she needs from us." Needless to say, I found this very moving.

It is important to remember that to heal does not always mean to cure.

Sometimes healing means that the person concerned will be helped to come to the end of their earthly life with grace and even joy, and with the minimum of suffering. It is hard for family, close friends, partners to accept that praying for somebody's recovery may not be their best interests. In such situations, perhaps we should pray that we are helped to transcend our own feelings if they are not for the highest good of the person we love.

As I suggested above, we can also ask Raphael for healing for groups, etc. If there is a problem in your town, perhaps antagonism between different groups of people, it would be good to gather a group of concerned and spiritually orientated people to meditate together and visualise a peaceful solution, though of course individual prayer or meditation does not go unheard.

WORKING WITH ARCHANGEL URIEL

It is perhaps easier to work with Uriel in practical ways than with any of the other Archangels, because there are many small but significant ways in which we can each help to prevent the climate changes, deforestation and other depredations that threaten our Planet. For example, individuals making private journeys, account for 60% of all travel in the United Kingdom and domestic use contributes more to the overproduction of greenhouse gasses than industry. This may sound depressing, but in fact it is encouraging because it means that even the small actions that we can take as individuals really do have an effect. If we are causing the problem, then the solutions lies in our hands.

We do still need to put pressure on our governments and the large corporations to change their policies, but we can do so in the knowledge that our personal actions are genuinely effective.

I know that many people reading this book will already be very well aware of ways in which they can reduce their "footprint" on the Earth, but the following list may be useful as an aide-memoire:

FOOD:
Buy local produce whenever possible to avoid the pollution caused by transporting food thousands of miles by road and air.

Did you know that one kiwi fruit flown from New Zealand to the

U.K. or the U.S.A. will create five times its own weight in carbon dioxide emissions?

(You don't have to go without kiwis - there are plenty of growers nearer to home.)

Buy organic foods whenever you can in order to reduce the damage done to the soil by agricultural chemicals. Yes, it probably costs a little more, but did you know that removing pesticides, nitrates and phosphates from our water supplies costs U.K. taxpayers over one billion pounds a year? That makes organic food look quite a bargain.

Look for farmers' markets. They are a good source of organic and unusual products and the produce will be local, fresh and usually cheaper than in supermarkets.

Avoid out-of-season fruits and vegetables - they have probably been grown as cash-crops in developing countries instead of food to feed the indigenous people.

Look out for food products from fair trade organizations.

Avoid foodstuffs with unnecessary packaging.

CLOTHES:

Avoid exploiting Third World workers. An incredibly cheap garment has probably been made by underpaid sweatshop workers and transported thousands of miles. Read labels. Ask questions.

Buy good quality clothes during Sales - they last longer than mid-price items and reduce waste.

Recycle. Swap. Scour the charity shops.

Make your own.

Buy clothes from fair trade companies wherever possible.

Choose natural fibers: cotton, linen, wool, silk and hemp, rather than synthetics which are often side-products of the polluting petro-chemical industry.

Look for organic sources of such fibers whenever possible.

HOUSEHOLD CHEMICALS:

Think about the impact household products have on the environment as well as your own health and that of your family.

Avoid chlorine bleach which pollutes rivers - use an alternative.

Buy "eco-friendly" products wherever possible. Read labels.

Ban chemicals from your garden. Go organic.

ENERGY:

When buying new household appliances choose energy-efficient ones. They may be dearer initially, but will soon save the difference through lower consumption.

Turn off electrical appliances when not in use: computers and television sets left on "standby" consume far more electricity than you might think.

Turn down the thermostat. Insulate your home. Wear another sweater!

Try to find "green" energy suppliers.

If you have a loft, make sure it is properly insulated.

If you have cavity walls, get them filled.

Consider installing solar panels and using innovative building materials.

TRANSPORT:

Is your car a gas-guzzler? Trade it in for a less polluting model.

Share car journeys and only drive if you really have to.

Ask yourself: Do I need a car at all?

Use public transport when you can. The more we use it, the better funding it will get and the better services we will receive.

Walk whenever possible - it will do your body good as well as your soul!

Think hard before flying. Could you make the journey by any other means?

Short-haul flights are the worst polluters, so finding alternatives is often relatively easy.

RECYCLING:

Recycle everything you can - paper, card, plastic, glass, tins, textiles, etc.

Buy recycled products whenever possible.

Buy goods with minimal packaging so that there is less to recycle.

If you have a garden, make and really use a compost heap.

If you haven't, there are neighborhood composting schemes in many places.

If your local authority does not have one already, agitate until they do.

Sell unwanted clothes, linens, furniture, household goods, etc., or give them to charities. Don't just throw them away.

And do all these things with awareness, holding the Archangel Uriel in your consciousness as you do so.

Finally, in case that all sounds rather grim and demanding, remember that Uriel delights in the beauty of the Earth and reminds us to do so too.

Sit by a river, climb a mountain, walk in a forest, swim in the sea, tend a garden, gaze at a magnificent sunset. Marvel at the iridescent beauty of a dragonfly and let it remind you of the immeasurably greater beauty of the angels.

See " a world in a grain of sand, and a heaven in a wild flower" as William Blake reminds us. Get out into the natural world as often as possible, especially if you are a city dweller. Seek out the parks and green spaces in your town and make the most of them.

Enjoy!

PART FOUR

ANGEL MESSAGES

ANGEL MESSAGES

The following messages were received as various times over a period of several months. The process began when I was receiving healing on a regular basis and the healer suggested that I should try to contact certain Angels.

She in turn was directed during the healing sessions as to which Angel I should ask for guidance.

I decided to use the journaling technique which I have described elsewhere in the book, and immediately began to get clear and often very moving messages. Initially, they came only when I sat down with the intention of recording any guidance I might receive. I did this at specific times and only asked for guidance from the Angels towards whom the healer had directed me. After a while, though, I began to get messages at unexpected times - such as when I was working on a painting, taking a bath or in the middle of washing the dishes! As I have said more than once, Angels do have a sense of humor!

Some of these messages were clearly guidance on personal issues and are not included here but others seemed to have much wider relevance and these latter I have included in the following pages. The format in which they were given to me was almost always similar: there would be some lines that described the "personality" or energy of the Angel, or said something general about the issue in question followed by much more specific guidance.

In transcribing my initial rapid scrawls I have separated the two parts of each transmission, though in fact they can usually be distinguished by a change of style. Sometimes I received impressions that were not put into words, and these I have added as notes at the end of the actual transmissions.

What fascinated me - and absolutely convinced me from the start that these writings were not coming from my own mind - was that the style and manner of expression of each Angel was not only different from my usual way of writing, but that each of them was quite distinct from all the others.

I feel extraordinarily blessed to have been given these message and to be able to share them with you. I hope you will find among them something of value in your own life.

THE ANGEL OF ABUNDANCE

There is no virtue in poverty, nor is there wrong in riches, provided always that you share your abundance and use it wisely.

Do not squander the gifts of the Earth, nor those of Heaven.

THE ANGEL OF CREATIVITY

All creativity flows from the Divine Source. Like a great fountain it flows without cease. Nothing can stem its flow, no drought can diminish it. It nourishes the Earth and all her creatures.

My work is to remind you of that, to maintain your connection to the Divine Source. I am a channel for the Divine. Through me Creativity can flow from the Source to all humanity, for every human soul is a creator.

I say to you:

When you lose sight of the Source you feel bereft. When your creativity is not flowing your soul becomes parched. Allow the unquenchable fountain of the Divine to nourish and nurture your soul. Allow me to bring that nourishment within your reach. Make yourself a clear channel that the life-giving water can flow through and you will never thirst.

Remember that she who bakes a cake is as much a creator as the finest sculptor, the most inspired composer. To fashion a dress, to make a garden, to bring a child lovingly into the world are all acts of creation and in God's eyes all are of equal merit.

THE ANGEL
OF RESPONSIBILITY

I am responsible. I do not impose burdens on you, but share those you find too heavy.

Your responsibilities may indeed feel too heavy to bear, but remember that God never gives any soul more responsibility than they can carry. That is why I am ever-present to lift the weight from your shoulders if ever it should feel too great. If you have been chosen to carry great responsibility it is because God knows that you are capable of doing so. Feel honored!

I say to you:

You don't have to be responsible all the time! In fact, it is somewhat big-headed to imagine that things will fall apart if you don't take responsibility for them all the time. Just remember that the Angels never take time off - so that you can!

I am respons-able: I respond.

Call on me and I will respond whenever you feel bowed down by earthly burdens. I will make them lighter. I will give you strength and patience ... and a sense of humor! Remember that "Angels can fly because they take themselves lightly."

THE ANGEL
OF GENTLENESS

I am as soft as a feather drifting on a windless day, as soft as a cloud that is not yet laden with rain. Rose petals resemble me, yet I have more strength than rock or steel.

With gentleness I accomplish what no army can achieve. I soften hardened hearts and help them to grow, I enter closed minds and help them to open. I bring healing where there has been violence, calm where there has been distress.

I say to you:

Do not think you can achieve everything by striving and effort. You will exhaust yourself without cause. All that you have to do, do gently. Everyone that crosses your path, receive with gentleness. Obstacles that seemed insurmountable before will melt away before you, solutions will appear to the thorniest of problems.

Be gentle with yourself. I say again, first and foremost be gentle with yourself. When you treat yourself harshly your own gentle self suffers and I suffer to see you so. Be not harsh in judgment against yourself. When you are gentle to yourself you become more able to be gentle to others.

Do not impose impossible tasks on yourself, or approach your work as if it were a challenge. When you work with gentleness, all your task are accomplished with ease. Nobody said that "gentle" had to mean "slow"!

Gently the flower opens, gently the day dawns.

Let me lead you softly by the hand, let me touch your mind and heart with love. For the other name of gentleness is Love.

THE ANGEL OF SPEED

Speed is an illusion. Time is an illusion. In the Angelic realms they are both meaningless, because we dwell in eternity even though our actions are instantaneous. Angels move at the speed of thought, but without any sensation of haste or change of time or place. In every moment we are both immediate and eternal. It is only through our deep desire to help those in human form that we have come to understand the concept of speed.

I say to you:

Speed is relative. When you have been immobile, any movement feels fast!

When you are not fulfilling your true purpose time weights heavily upon you, but when you engage in what you love, enjoy and know to be your true work, time becomes as meaningless to you as it to us.

Do not feel limited by time. Do what you deeply desire and the time for doing it will become manifest. Understand time as another gift of Abundance - there is enough time for EVERYTHING.

Do not work in haste, nor feel guilt about the speed at which you accomplish any task.

Light is eternal. You are eternal. Hasten only in your journey towards the Light.

NOTES

Apart from the Angel's words, I received some strong impressions that were not expressed verbally. First, that this Angel is female. Second, that she has only been given the name "Angel of Speed" and the responsibility for overlighting our behavior in relation to speed, in recent time, and because speed has become so damaging on Earth. Third, that she may also be the Angel of Time, or that the Angel of Time has taken on this new, additional role and the understanding of the concept of speed, because humanity needs so much help in this area.

THE ANGEL
OF REST

In six days God created Heaven and Earth and everything that in them is, and on the seventh day She rested from her labors.

Why should you be any different?

NOTES

Well, she didn't waste any words! I had a strong impression of a rather nannyish personality, almost as if she were saying "Come along now, off to bed with you."

THE ANGEL
OF HOPE

Hope sustains us through the darkest times of our lives. When the fog of despair is so thick that we cannot even imagine the way forward, Hope brings a light which enables us to put one foot in front of the other, again and again, without stumbling, until we reach the greater Light.

Hope can sustain life itself when, by all human reckoning, that is not possible. Yet, consider how in your everyday speech you deny this power.

You say, "Well, I hope it will be O.K." when you know for certain that "it" (whatever it is) will not. "I hope you don't mind," when you know that you are causing offence. Or, "I hope I'll get there in time," when you have set out too late.

Your denial can in no way diminish the power of the Angel of

Hope, for your puny speech is no threat to his might. What you do is to deny yourselves. As long as you speak of Hope in a weak and confusing way, you close your minds and hearts to the power, the strength, the sustenance and support of mighty Hope.

Open your hearts to Hope. Open your minds to the reality of Hope. Be ready to receive the blessings of Hope. Reach out to Hope and he will lift you out of the blackness and bleakness of despair and show you the Light.

Hope. Dare to hope! Dare to hope that you will be fulfilled, that your wishes and dreams will be met, as well as your needs.

Hope, even when you cannot see the way ahead. I will bring a light to show you the way.

Remember my power, and hope with strength and with energy. Be vigorous in hoping! Remember that Hope is an action, not a vague sentiment. Be disciplined in hoping - keep at it. Do not give up. Work actively with me and I will work with you.

NOTES

I had the impression of a Being of immense power. A masculine energy, a Being of towering dimensions.

THE ANGEL OF SIMPLICITY

The life of Angels is simple because we dwell in Spirit. We commune in Spirit. We are Spirit.

We understand the difficulties humanity encounters, through the need to maintain the physical body with food, clothing and shelter, the need to provide financially for these necessities, the need for companionship and emotional comfort, and we have compassion for them. Admiration too, for the choice to incarnate on Earth is a courageous one, and there are many at this time who have made that choice in the spirit of service.

Yet, we also observe that those in human form create even more difficulty for themselves through their desire for more than they truly need.

I say to you, simplify your life!

Discard that which is not necessary, be it material or mental. Do not hoard outgrown thought any more than you would keep outworn clothes. Do not maintain friendships that are not appropriate to your life now. Do not surround yourself with superfluous tasks any more than with excess possessions.

Seek that which is essential to the life of the Spirit as well as the body and know that all your true needs will be met.

APPENDIX
USEFUL CONTACTS

ANGEL WEB-SITES: U.K.

www.angelart.me.uk

The author's website. Details of talks, workshops, paintings, cards, exhibitions, etc.

www.angellight.co.uk

The website of Chrissie Astell, angel author and workshop leader.

www.soulschool.co.uk

Details of Theolyn Cortens' workshops, talks, courses and books.

www.worldangelday.com

Details of World Angel Day annual events.

www.sanctuaryofangels.com

Details of courses, etc.

www.spiritual-connections

Details of workshops, etc.

ANGEL WEB-SITES: USA

www.angeltherapy.com

Doreen Virtue's Angel website. Details of talks, workshops, etc.

www.angelslove.net

Sherry Whitfield Merrell's website. Information on workshops in USA and Canada, study and support groups.

www.lindasonnet.com

The website of Linda Sonnet Carlson. Workshops, newsletter, etc.

www.angelenergyhealing.com

Workshops in USA and Ireland

www.spiritualsymphony.com

Workshops and conferences in USA

OTHER RELEVANT WEB-SITES

www.worldpuja.com

Project organizing meditations for world peace.

www.music-in-hospitals.org.uk

information about healing through music.

www.paintingsinhospitals.org.uk

information about art in hospitals

FREE ANGEL CARDS

The color illustrations in this book have been reproduced as greeting cards. For a free card, send a stamped, addressed envelope at least 15 x 19 cms (5.5 x 7.5 ins) to:

ANGEL ART, P.O. Box 172 TOTNES, Devon, TQ9 9AD, U.K.

(Readers outside the U.K., please send an addressed envelope and an International Reply Coupon.)

Please mention which illustration you would like.

BIBIBLIOGRAPHY AND SUGGESTED FURTHER READING

Astell, Christine, *Discovering Angels,* Duncan Baird, London 2005

Astell, Christine, *Advice from Angels*, Godsfield, London 2005

Cortens, Theolyn. *Living With Angels,* Piatkus, London 2003

Davidson, Gustav. *A Dictionary of Angels,* Macmillan, N.Y. 1967

Fox, Matthew and Sheldrake, Rupert. *The Physics of Angels,* Harper, S.Francisco 1996

Hickman, Leo. *A Life Stripped Bare,* Transworld, London 2005

Israel, Martin *Angels, Messengers of Grace*, SPCK, London 1995

Moolenburg, H.C. *A Handbook of Angels,* C.W. Daniel, Saffron Walden 1988

Moolenburg, H.C. *Meetings with Angels,* C.W. Daniel, Saffron Walden 1992

Smith, P. & G. *Meditation, a Treasury of Technique,* C.W. Daniel, Saffron Walden 1989

Underhill, James. *Angels,* Element, Shaftesbury 1994

Virtue, Doreen. *Archangels and, Ascended Masters,* Hay House. Ca. 2003

Wilson, Peter Lamborn. *Angels,* Thames & Hudson, London 1980

O

is a symbol of the world,
of oneness and unity. O Books
explores the many paths of wholeness
and spiritual understanding which
different traditions have developed down
the ages. It aims to bring this knowledge
in accessible form, to a general readership,
providing practical spirituality to today's seekers.

For the full list of over 200 titles covering:

- CHILDREN'S PRAYER, NOVELTY AND GIFT BOOKS
- CHILDREN'S CHRISTIAN AND SPIRITUALITY
- CHRISTMAS AND EASTER
- RELIGION/PHILOSOPHY
- SCHOOL TITLES
- ANGELS/CHANNELLING
- HEALING/MEDITATION
- SELF-HELP/RELATIONSHIPS
- ASTROLOGY/NUMEROLOGY
- SPIRITUAL ENQUIRY
- CHRISTIANITY, EVANGELICAL
  AND LIBERAL/RADICAL
- CURRENT AFFAIRS
- HISTORY/BIOGRAPHY
- INSPIRATIONAL/DEVOTIONAL
- WORLD RELIGIONS/INTERFAITH
- BIOGRAPHY AND FICTION
- BIBLE AND REFERENCE
- SCIENCE/PSYCHOLOGY

Please visit our website,
www.O-books.net

Crystal Prescriptions
Judy Hall

This symptom-based A-Z directory by Judy Hall, author of the best-selling *The Crystal Bible*, will help you to identify exactly the right crystal for your needs, whether for healing of mind, body, psyche or spirit. It will point you to useful stones for improving vitality and well-being, and for balancing the chakras. Listing over 1,200 "symptoms", it is a practical first-aid guide based on sound crystal healing principles that have been practised for millennia. Crystals are a gentle, non-invasive system of holistic healing with no side effects. Suitable for children and animals, crystals can also benefit the environment and your home.

An internationally known author, astrologer, psychic, healer and workshop leader, Judy has been a karmic counsellor for over thirty years. Her books have been translated into fifteen languages. Her most recent is Torn Clouds (O Books).

1 905047 40 1
£7.99/$15.95

Divine Astrology: the Cosmic Religion
Enlisting the Aid of the Planetary Powers
Lyn Birkbeck

Most of what has been written in the name of astrology refers to personality and prediction. *Divine Astrology* presents Astrology in its true sense as a spiritual rather than predictive system. It sees personality as being an expression of Spirit, and life as being a journey of Spirit driven by cosmic forces and governed by definite laws. Seen in this way the user is no longer simply a hapless puppet of the astrological influences prevailing at birth and through life. He or she is seen as an entity who can become en rapport with the very energies that are the stuff of astrology, the Planetary Powers. It relates these to the nature of God, to other religions and to modern cosmology and physics. We are co-creators with God, and by communing with the Hands of God, the Planetary Powers, we can change our destiny for the better.

To this end, *Divine Astrology* first equips the reader with the "Scriptures", the planets, Signs and Houses that tell what forces we are all subject to. But we are direct expressions of these Powers and Conditions, and so are able to commune with them. This paves the way for the esoteric teaching that we are able to become as Gods. It leads onto the "Rituals" that are the Practice of Astrology, the Cosmic Religion. Like any religion, this involves prayer and ceremony, but more precisely "Invocation". The "equipment" of these Rituals are the 40 Cards that come with the book. The seeker is shown ways to resolve problems, have questions answered, attain support and security, receive enlightenment, become empowered.

The book closes with "God's Skywriting" which demonstrates in simple tabular form how all the major events of the 20th and early 21st Century are correlated to the Cycles of various Planetary Pairs. It shows us how we are all caught up in something far greater and more universal than we usually believe.

For *The Instant Astrologer*

Lyn is one of those rare astrologers who combines profound personal

information with an accessible style designed to empower his readers to do it for themselves. This ground-breaking combination of software and book will enable people to look deeply into themselves and their relationships with others. Lyn knows the magic that comes from giving people the freedom to follow their own investigations.
RICHARD BEAUMONT, *Kindred Spirit*

The brilliant Lyn Birkbeck's new book and CD package, The Instant Astrologer, *combines modern technology with the wisdom of the ancients, creating an invitation to enlightenment for the masses, just when we need it most!*
JENNY LYNCH, *Host of NYC's StarPower Astrology Television Show*

Lyn Birkbeck began his working life as a musician and record producer and has now been a widely-consulted astrologer for over 20 years. He is the best-selling author of *Do It Yourself Astrology, The Astrological Oracle, The Instant Astrologer*, and *Astro-Wisdom,* and lives in the Lake District, England.

1 90547 03 7
£14.99/$24.9

Past Life Angels
Discovering Your Life's Master-plan
Jenny Smedley

Everyone knows about the existence of Angels, but this book reveals the discovery of a very special and previously unsuspected legion- that of Past Life Angels. These beings are not only here and now; they have been with us through all our lives, since our soul's creation. They are still there to nudge us, guide us and jog our memories. The clues are there, and by following them we can kick our higher self into operation, and change our lives beyond recognition.

When we connect with our Past Life Angels we no longer drift through life uncertain of who we really are and what we should be doing. Our instincts are right-our lives are unfinished business. Our soul is eternal, and has a job to do in this life. It has a master plan that has evolved through all our lifetimes.

For the first time, Jenny Smedley shows why your past lives are important to your future and how they can change your current one. She discusses the contracts made before this birth, both with others and yourself. She explains the illnesses and fears we suffer from, and, above all, how we can stick to the right path with the help of our Past Life Angels, once we have found it.

Waste no more time on your spiritual path, read this book and be inspired, awakened and ready to run where others walk; I wish it were around when I was ignoring those nudges and stumbling through life's lessons!
DAVID WELLS, Astrologer and Medium

Jenny Smedley has done it again and created an excellent book which helps you in this life, and the next. I work with my own angels every day but this book has shown me a new avenue to explore. Learn how your angels can hep you with your current life challenges using the assistance of your past life angels. Jenny certainly knows her stuff, and her many fans will not be disappointed.
JACKY NEWCOMB, angel teacher, columnist, presenter and author of *An Angel Treasury*

Jenny Smedley, columnist and writer, has condensed ten years experience and research into this book. A guest speaker on hundreds of radio and TV shows worldwide, she wrote it in response to the many requests she gets on how we can find that *something* that's missing from our lives.

1 905047 31 2
£9.99/$16.95

Savage Breast

One Man's Search for the Goddess
Tim Ward

We think of God as male, but the most common representation of the divine through our history has been as female, as the Goddess. When did this major change happen, and why? More importantly, what did it do to our psyches, and what does it mean for present day relationships between men and women?

Facing the Goddess unleashes turbulent emotions for Ward. With frank honesty he describes the traumas that erupt in his relationship with the woman he loves, who accompanied him on many of his journeys. He weaves travelogue, archaeology, history, art, autobiography into a fascinating and gripping journey through the depths of our history and minds.

An epic, elegant, scholarly search for the goddess, weaving together travel, Greek mythology, and personal autobiographic relationships into a remarkable exploration of the Western World's culture and sexual history. It is also entertainingly human, as we listen and learn from this accomplished person and the challenging mate he wooed. If you ever travel to Greece, take Savage Breast along with you.

HAROLD SCHULMAN, Professor of Gynaecology at Winthrop University Hospital, and author of *An Intimate History of the Vagina.*

Few male writers except theologians have dared to interpret the goddess movement but Tim Ward in his frank, intrepid way, has given us a thoughtful, personal account of one man's look at the goddess and why many men have been so angry at women.

SUSAN SWAN, author of *What Cassanova Told Me.*

Ward's book is a kind of archaeology of the soul. He digs through the layers of his own male psyche and cultural conditioning, and does not flinch at what he finds buried underneath. He brings ancient rituals to life as he re-imagines what it must have been like to be a man living in the time of the Goddess. His vivid account cuts to the heart of man's relationship with the feminine divine – and, even more important, to men's relationships with flesh-and-blood women.

WADE DAVIS, author of *One River,* and *The Serpent and the Rainbow.*

Weaving the mythic into the everyday, this book is a fascinating and honest exploration of one man's venture into the realms of the divine feminine. A modern-day Odyssey, a rich travelogue of interior and exterior dimensions, Savage Breast is a valuable contribution to not only understanding but experiencing the spirit of unity.

LUCINDA VARDEY, author of *God in All Worlds,* and *The Flowering of the Soul.*

A brutally honest and passionate account of one man's odyssey as he

searches to reconcile himself with the goddess, ie; the mysterious yet all powerful feminine principle so deeply rooted in each of us.
Tom Harpur, author of *The Pagan Christ*.

Savage Breast *is a powerful account of one man's relationship with the ancient goddesses of Europe. Tim Ward's personal encounters with the goddesses' statues, frescos, temples and sacred sites remind us that these artefacts are not sterile stones but the touchstones to a still living world of human experience.*
RICHARD RUDGLEY, author of *Lost Civilizations of the Stone Age*.

Savage Breast *is ballsy, entertaining, adventuresome, wild, scholarly, sexy, and deep.*
HELEN KNODE, author of *The Ticket Out*.

A fascinating and fearless exploration of the Goddess and her attributes, for men and women alike. Tim Ward's bold exploration of sexuality in all its guises is an inspiration—frightening, funny, intoxicating (sexy!), always illuminating.
JAMES O'REILLY, publisher, *Travelers' Tales*.

Tim Ward studied philosophy at the University of British Columbia and lived in Asia for six years. He wrote three books about his experiences in the Far East, including the best selling *What the Buddha Never Taught*. He now teaches communications courses based in Maryland, and continues to travel globally.

1 905047 58 4
£12.99 $20.95

Soul Power
Nikki de Carteret

How do you create inner stability in times of chaos? How do you cultivate the power of presence? Where does humility meet mastery? These are just some of the threads of spiritual inquiry that Nikki weaves into a tapestry of Soul Power. Juxtaposing fascinating teachings from the ancient mystics with stories of modern seekers, as well as her own extraordinary journey towards wholeness, she invites you to explore the factors that drain your spiritual energy, and what transformational forces restore it.

I have, quite simply, never before read a book that made me feel so keenly the love of God.
JOY PARKER, author of *Woman Who Glows in the Dark.*

A beautiful and touching expression of the spiritual journey.
BARBARA SHIPKA, author of *Leadership in a Challenging World.*

A unique combination of scholarly research and hands-on experience.
MICHAEL RYMER, Hollywood film director

Nikki de Carteret holds a master's degree from the Sorbonne in medieval mystic literature and leads workshops around the world on personal and organizational transformation.

1 903816 17 3
£9.99 $14.95